Dream of Legacy

Dream of Legacy

RAISING STRONG AND FINANCIALLY SECURE BLACK KIDS

Anne-Lyse Wealth

Copyright @ Dream of Legacy, LLC.

All rights reserved. No part of this publication may be reproduced, distributed, or transmitted in any form or by any means, including photocopying, recording, or other electronic or mechanical methods, without the publisher's prior written permission.

Front cover design by Karine Zekam Toka

First printing edition 2020.
Dream of Legacy, LLC.
www.dreamoflegacy.com

Limit of liability: All content reflects the author's opinion. The information in this book should not be misconstrued for professional financial, accounting, or legal advice. Although the author and publisher have made reasonable efforts to ensure that the contents of this book are correct at press time, the author and publisher do not make and disclaim any representations and warranties regarding the content of the book, whether expressed or implied. The author and publisher hereby disclaim any liability to any party for any loss, damage, or cost arising from or related to the book's content. Neither the author, nor the publisher should be held liable or responsible to any person or entity concerning any loss or incidental, indirect, or consequential damages caused, or alleged to have been caused directly, or indirectly, by the contents contained herein.

*This book is dedicated to my sisters: Dr. Z and Aurore.
Thank you for loving me and helping raise me.
I know that we will reunite one day. Until then, thank you for watching over the family.
I will love you forever, in this life and the next.*

Contents

	Prologue · ix
Chapter 1	Black Privilege · 1 Unlocking the greatness in your DNA · 1
Chapter 2	Teaching Self-Love · 7 Building your Kings and Queens up early so nobody can tear them down · 7
Chapter 3	Teaching Gratitude and Positive Thinking · 12 Coaching children to appreciate what they have, and to embrace positivity · 12
Chapter 4	Teaching Solid Financial Habits Early · 16 Teaching young kids the key fundamentals of money · · · · · · · · · · · · · · · · 16
Chapter 5	Assessing Your Financial Health · 20 Taking a snapshot of your financial situation · 20
Chapter 6	Optimizing Your Credit Strategy · 24 Using credit to your advantage · 24
Chapter 7	Making the Most of Your Income · 31 Learning to stretch your income · 31

Chapter 8	Managing Debt······································· 37
	Understanding the fundamentals of debt ··············· 37
Chapter 9	Saving for the Near Future ···························· 56
	Building solid short and medium-term saving strategies············· 56
Chapter 10	Saving for the Long Run································ 62
	Building a successful long-term saving strategy ············ 62
Chapter 11	Work Ethic and Entrepreneurship ······················106
	Teaching children the value of hard work·················106
Chapter 12	Building Multiple Sources of Income ···················110
	Increasing your income streams························110
Chapter 13	Estate Planning······································112
	Organizing your affairs for your loved ones ···············112
Chapter 14	The Power of Community ·····························122
	Understanding the importance of coming together ···········122
Chapter 15	Key Financial Mistakes to Avoid························127
	Avoiding common obstacles to financial success ···········127
	Final Thoughts ······································135
	Acknowledgments····································137
	Notes ··139
	About the Author ····································143

Prologue

Juneteenth, June 19, 1865, marks the effective end of slavery in the United States of America. One hundred and fifty-five years later, the racial wealth disparity continues to widen in the country.

In 2016, the median White family in the United States had more than ten times the wealth of the median Black family.[I]

An even more significant concern is the 54 percent growth of the racial wealth gap between Black and White families between 1992 and 2016—from 100,000 dollars to 154,000 dollars.

During the eighty-nine years after the United States Declaration of Independence, White Americans accumulated wealth while African Americans were left to fend for themselves. In 1865, the United States Congress ratified the 13th Amendment to abolish slavery, though it was still legal as a punishment for a crime. Close to four million enslaved Black Americans were set free. While slave owners received monetary compensation for losing "property," enslaved Americans were released without being given a fair shot at success. Without any possessions or even a place to stay, they were one crime away from being legally subjected to involuntary servitude. Due to systemic racism, social and economic racial disparities continued to grow.

In the 1930s, the Home Owners' Loan Corporation, a government-sponsored corporation, began to identify the safety level of real estate investments in hundreds of cities across the United States. That is when "redlining" began—a practice consisting of marking in red areas with significant Black populations on security maps. The Federal Housing Administration, which was created around the same time to insure mortgage companies, banks, and other lenders, did not insure mortgages in redline areas for being too "risky." As a result of redlining, most Black Americans did not have access to home loans, and the racial disparity in home ownership and wealth increased.[II]

During the 1980s, as the crack epidemic destroyed Black neighborhoods, lawmakers passed a series of legislations that continued to increase racial inequalities in the United States.

For instance, the Anti-Drug Abuse Act of 1986 created a "100 to 1" disparity between crack and powder cocaine—two forms of the same drug.* Subsequently, the Violent Crime Control and Law Enforcement Act was passed in 1994. The "1994 Crime Bill", which aimed to be tougher on crime, resulted in higher mass incarceration of Black and Latino men compared to White men.†°

One hundred and fifty-five years after the 13th Amendment, Black people in America still suffer from the consequences of White supremacy. In 2020, institutional racism still plagues the country, more specifically the Black community. Black people continue to face discrimination in the hiring process, wage earning, access to education, healthcare, or the criminal justice system, to name a few.

The African American problem is very similar to the African problem.

Though Africans remained on the continent and were not enslaved in the Western world, every country in Africa, except Liberia and Ethiopia, suffered from a different kind of evil—colonization.

Between the 1870s and 1900s, most countries in Africa were taken over by European colonization. Colonialism generated wealth for Europe by stripping African countries of their resources, cultures, religions, and political identities. It was not until 1977 that colonialism ended in all parts of Africa. However, to this day, Africans still suffer from the economic and psychological consequences of colonialism. Some Western countries continue to maintain their position in Africa by practicing modern-day colonialism using exploitation and political turmoil.

In most countries, Black people are at the bottom of the totem pole. Much like African Americans in the United States, in many parts of Africa, Africans are treated as second-class citizens.

---

* Crack cocaine was mainly prevalent in Black neighborhoods. The 1986 Anti-Drug Act mandated a minimum of five years of prison for the possession of five grams of crack cocaine or more as opposed to five hundred grams of powder cocaine. After twenty-four years, with the Fair Sentencing Act in 2010, the disparity between crack cocaine and powder cocaine didn't disappear. But it was reduced to a ratio of eighteen to one.

† ° According to the 2018 "Report to the United Nations on Racial Disparities in the US Criminal Justice System," by the Sentencing Project, African Americans are 5.9 times more likely to be incarcerated than White Americans, and Hispanic Americans are 3.1 times more likely to be incarcerated. Also, African Americans and Hispanic Americans comprise 29 percent of the US population. But, they make up 57 percent of the US prison population. The Sentencing Project is a nonprofit organization working to reduce the use of incarceration and address racial disparities in the criminal justice system in the United States.

The Black experience is unique. Generational wealth is not yet common around the Black community. Most of us do not have access to financial education.

One can easily judge the financial decisions made by someone coming from poverty. However, the need that many Black people have to display their wealth once they reach a level of success can be explained by our history as people. It is less a reflection of who we are as a people than it is the consequence of the struggle we experience as a constanty marginalized group of society. Often, Black people who were able to escape poverty, have a desire to celebrate by spending the wealth they have built. Knowing where most of us come from, it is almost a natural reaction to overindulge financially.

When you add to that the fact of continually being undervalued by society, it is easy to fall into the trap of associating your value or self-worth to material possessions. As a result, we often buy things we used to dream of having in our youth to make ourselves feel better.

I am the youngest of five kids. My parents grew up with modest means and were able to achieve financial independence (the point at which one has enough passive income to cover their baseline living expenses) at an early age. My father started his career as a pharmacist, and my mother as a medical doctor. Over the years, my parents built a significant real estate portfolio. They bought a house in the late 1970s and still live in that house forty years later. My parents were financially comfortable, but they were never excessive in how much money they spent. They provided a good living for our family of eight, as well as for several extended family members. However, they always lived considerably below their means. My parents did not care much about exterior signs of riches. They did not feel the need to keep up with the Joneses. They saved, on average, 50 percent of their income. My dad could afford to buy a new car, yet he chose to drive the same car for twenty years, while his friends were buying new cars every few years.

My parents' choice of a moderate lifestyle has served them well over the years. When I was younger, my dad was ripped off by a trusted business partner of a considerable amount of money. Because my parents were living below their means, our lifestyles were not affected. My parents were able to weather that financial storm. It was not until many years later that I understood the seriousness of the situation they had faced.

Approximately five years ago, my mother was diagnosed with a long-term illness. As her disease progressed quickly, she had to retire from her career as a medical doctor earlier than she intended to. For the past few years, my mother has required round-the-clock medical care—which comes at a high financial cost. We could not have predicted how fast my mother's health would deteriorate. However, my parents were prepared to face the unexpected expenses associated with my mother's care because they had chosen to live below their means for decades.

These examples highlight the importance of saving and being financially secure. It helps you prepare for the unexpected.

I attribute my parents' journey to financial independence to their ability to be comfortable in their shoes, no matter their material possessions. They did not attach their self-worth to the things they possessed. Money gave them freedom. They had money, but money never had them. I believe that is a quality we should all try to instill in our children to set them on a path to building real financial security.

We need to embrace our origins, struggles, successes, and challenges as a Community. All of those characteristics are part of our heritage. We should teach our kids pride in who they are, their rich heritage as part of the Black community. If we diligently do that, their self-worth will not be attached to how well they are doing financially or be affected by material possessions. Our Kings and Queens will grow up comfortable in their shoes. They will feel rich, and the need to flaunt their wealth will be considerably curved. There is a fine line between indulging and wasting money to the point of failing to build your long-term financial future. That is a lesson we need to teach our kids so they can grow up striving for financial independence.

I wrote this book to give current and future parents tools to help raise strong, proud, and financially savvy children. My hope is that our Kings and Queens grow up with the mindset to set their families on the path to true financial independence. I believe that this book can inspire and empower the Black community one child at a time and create generations of financially and socially responsible Black millionaires.

CHAPTER 1
Black Privilege
Unlocking the greatness in your DNA

Ancient Egypt, previously known as Kemet, "the Black Land," is home to one of the oldest civilizations on Earth, which can be traced back to approximately 3000 Before the Common Era (B.C.E.). It was an independent nation where some of the most significant scientific and technological advancements originated.

For close to a millennium, Ancient Egypt was a prosperous state with unparalleled wealth. However, around 2200 B.C.E., Egypt, as an ancient civilization started to decline until its eventual demise around 30 B.C.E.—when it became a province of the Roman Empire. There is evidence of foreign invasions, such as the Persian or the Greek Empires, civil wars, as well as a severe and long-term drought that partially explain what happened. However, there are still a lot of questions regarding the decline of Ancient Egypt. To this day, there are remnants of the creations left behind by the people of Ancient Egypt, including temples, hieroglyphs, and pyramids.

The great pyramid of Giza is the largest Egyptian pyramid ever built. It is the oldest of the Seven Wonders of the Ancient World and the only one to have survived close to five thousand years later.

The grandeur of the creations of the people of Ancient Egypt should serve as a constant reminder of what we are capable of as a Community.

King Mansa Musa was an Emperor of the Mali Empire in West Africa in the fourteenth century. Under his rule, the Empire grew to include a significant portion of West Africa. He was the first African ruler to be known throughout Europe and the Middle East after setting out on a pilgrimage to Mecca. After his pilgrimage, King Mansa Musa built schools, universities, libraries, and mosques in Timbuktu, Mali. He turned the city of Timbuktu into the center of culture and religious study it is today. In 1988, Timbuktu became a United Nations Educational, Scientific and Cultural Organization (UNESCO) World Heritage Site. King Mansa Musa is also known as the wealthiest person in history.

Those two examples are testimonies that greatness is a part of our DNA as African descendants.

In 1964, UNESCO formed the General History of Africa. The intent was to tell Africa's history by Africans, which would thus be free of colonization or slavery bias. The eleven-volume collection was the result of the collaboration of hundreds of historians whose work was overseen by an International Scientific Committee comprised of over 60 percent Africans. It is a resource to explore as we strive further to educate ourselves and our children on our African heritage. Telling stories to our children about their ancestors and their family members, and sharing the obstacles they overcame helps give them intergenerational strength and resilience.

We live in a world where Black people are considered second-class citizens. This vision of Black people is the same in most places I have visited throughout my life—from America to Europe, Asia, or even Africa. Being born Black means working twice as hard to get half as much as your White peers.

Black people around the world have overcome tremendous challenges over the years. We have been subjected to slavery, colonization, segregation, apartheid, and other inhumane conditions. Our oppressors worked hard at convincing us that a Black person was worth less than a White person. They attempted to strip us of our identity and divide us by highlighting our differences and encouraging us to develop hate for our physical features and our people.

In the United States, over the years, the Black community has continued to be disadvantaged by racially biased legislation and social policies. In Africa, the creation of unnatural colonial borders continued to divide Africans so they would focus on their differences instead of embracing their similarities.

DREAM OF LEGACY

For many years, those tactics contributed to the destruction of our communities. But throughout history, we had leaders like Sojourner Truth,[*] Nat Turner,[†] Frederick Douglass,[‡] Harriet Tubman,[§] Madam C.J. Walker,[¶] W.E.B. Du Bois,[**]

---

[*] Sojourner Truth was an American abolitionist and women's rights activist famous for her "Ain't I a Woman" speech on racial inequalities. She was born enslaved but escaped to freedom in 1826.

[†] Nat Turner was an enslaved man who led an effective rebellion of enslaved people in the United States of America in 1831. Turner was sentenced to death by hanging. He is an example of African Americans fighting against White oppression.

[‡] Frederick Douglass was a leader of the abolitionist movement, author, and public speaker who escaped slavery in 1838. Often called the father of the civil rights movement, he was also an advocate for women's rights.

[§] Harriet Tubman, "the Moses of her people," was an American abolitionist and political activist. She escaped slavery in the mid-1800s and subsequently helped dozens of enslaved people gain freedom as an "Underground Railroad" conductor. She was also the first African American woman to serve in the military, and the first woman to lead a military operation.

[¶] Madam C.J. Walker was a pioneer woman entrepreneur, philanthropist, and activist. She was the first woman self-made millionaire on record in the United States. She strived to empower women in the workforce and built her fortune by selling hair care products to Black women, starting in the early 1900s.

[**] William Edward Burghardt Du Bois, "W.E.B. Dubois," was an American civil rights activist, historian, and writer who co-founded the National Association for the Advancement of Colored People (NAACP) in 1909. He was the first African American to earn a doctorate from Harvard University in 1895.

Yaa Asantewaa,[*] Funmilayo Ransom Kuti,[†] Kwame Nkrumah,[‡] Rosa Parks,[§] Martin Luther King Jr.,[¶] and Malcolm X,[**]

---

[*] Yaa Asantewaa, known as "Queen Mother," was an Ashanti leader. She was an advocate for human rights and a leader against British colonization in what is now known as Ghana. She led the Yaa Asantewaa War of Independence against the British in the early 1900s. During the rebellion, she was captured and exiled to Seychelles until she died in 1921.
[†] Funmilayo Ransom Kuti was a Nigerian educator and activist in the anti-colonial movement in Nigeria. She was the leading advocate of women's rights in her country in the 1950s. She was also the mother of Fela Kuti, human rights activist and pioneer of the Afrobeat music genre.
[‡] Kwame Nkrumah was a Pan-Africanist who led Ghana (then the Gold Coast) to become the first African colony to gain independence in 1957. He became Ghana's first president. After Ghana gained independence, the country became the center of activity for the liberation of other African colonies.
[§] Rosa Parks was a civil rights activist who, in 1955, sat in the front of a bus in Montgomery, Alabama. At the time, the front of the bus was for White people only. Rosa Parks refused to give up her seat to White passengers. She also helped organize the year-long Montgomery Bus Boycott, which resulted in the Supreme Court ruling that segregation on public buses was unconstitutional.
[¶] Martin Luther King Jr. was a social activist, leader, and the face of the civil rights movement from the mid-1950s to his assassination in 1968. He founded the Southern Christian Leadership Conference (SCLC) in 1957 to help achieve equality for African Americans through nonviolent protest. He won the Nobel Peace Prize in 1964 and was assassinated in 1968. That year he had given a speech in Memphis on the economic empowerment of the Black community. In his speech, Dr. King emphasized the need for an economic Bill of Rights to bridge the economic gap between the haves and the have nots in America.
[**] Malcolm X was a leader of the civil rights movement advocating Black pride and Black nationalism. In 1964, he established the Organization of Afro American Unity (OAAU), a Pan-Africanist organization founded to fight for African Americans' rights and encourage cooperation between Africans and people of African descent. He was assassinated in 1965.

Patrice Lumumba,[*] Maya Angelou,[†] Nelson Mandela,[‡] Thurgood Marshall,[§] Thomas Sankara,[¶] and Barack Obama,[**] and many others who gave us a sense of pride and encouraged us to dream big and fight for our rights.

It is in our best interest to educate our children about the brilliant Black men and women that broke barriers and accomplished great things before them. We cannot rely on a biased school system to do so.

Black people are at the origin of many technological advancements, such as the automatic elevated doors invented by Alexander Miles, the first blood bank envisioned by Charles Richard Drew, the ironing board developed by Sarah Boone, the first gas mask or the three-position traffic signal both conceived by Garrett Morgan, and the first home security system designed by Mary Van Brittan Brown. These are only a few innovations by Black men and women that we can use to build our children's pride and inspire them to dream bigger.

---

[*] Patrice Lumumba was a revolutionary leader who became the first prime minister of what is now known as the Democratic Republic of Congo (DRC). He played a crucial role in its transformation from a Belgian colony to an independent Republic in 1960. He was a leader of the African liberation movement. Once called by Malcolm X, "the greatest Black man who ever walked the continent of Africa," Lumumba was assassinated in 1961.

[†] Maya Angelou was an American poet, actress, and civil rights activist. Through her social activism, she denounced the economic and racial oppression of the Black community.

[‡] Nelson Mandela was a leader of the antiapartheid movement in South Africa in the 1940s. He spent close to 30 years in prison for his activism and became the face of the movement. Upon release from prison in 1990, he decided to promote a message of peace in South Africa. He won the Nobel Peace Prize in 1993 and became South Africa's first Black president in 1994. He retired from politics in 1999 but continued his work as a peace and social activist.

[§] Thurgood Marshall was an American lawyer who became the first African American appointed on the Supreme Court in 1967. He argued and won countless cases in front of the United States Supreme Court, most notably *Brown v. Board of Education* in 1954.

[¶] Thomas Sankara was a political leader in Burkina Faso in the 1980s. He was a Pan-Africanist who believed that Burkina Faso could learn to sustain itself without foreign aid. He was a revolutionary who fought corruption and led Burkina Faso for four years. Thomas Sankara promoted public health, literacy, self-reliance, and the advancement of women. He was assassinated on October 15, 1987.

[**] Barack Obama was the first Black president of the United States of America. He revolutionized healthcare in the United States with the 2010 Affordable Care Act and allowed close to 90 percent of Americans to have healthcare insurance. He won the Nobel Peace Prize in 2009 and showed Black people throughout the world, especially our youth, that no dream is too big.

Black people have also been at the onset of many cultural trends from music (jazz,[*] rock and roll,[†] house,[‡] rumba,[§] afrobeat,[¶] or hip-hop[**]) and dance, to language, fashion, and aesthetics . . . to name a few. Though we do not always get the credit we deserve, Black people's contribution to society is immeasurable.

It is essential to teach our kids about our history so that they can feel the level of pride that should come from being part of a people that continue to strive and overcome the most horrendous circumstances. We must teach our youth about the privilege it is to be Black—before the world teaches them that it is a handicap. When we, as a people, understand that our ancestors' strength gives us superpowers, we will realize that Black is truly magic. Only then will we be secure in who we are and will we finally be able to achieve true financial success as a Community.

---

[*] Jazz originated in the African American communities of New Orleans between the end of the nineteenth century and the beginning of the twentieth century.

[†] Rock and roll gained popularity in the United States of America in the 1950s, deriving from rhythm and blues, which originated in the Black community.

[‡] House music originated at Club Warehouse on the Southside of Chicago in the 1970s. Frankie Knuckles, a black DJ at that club, known as the "Godfather of house music," would mix soul music with more rhythmic beats.

[§] Rumba was created in Cuba in the mid-nineteenth century by enslaved Africans as a way to protest.

[¶] Afrobeat was created in the 1960s as a blend of West African music, jazz, and funk rhythms.

[**] Hip-hop emerged as an underground movement in the late 1970s in the South Bronx, a predominantly African American community in New York City. In 2017, hip-hop replaced rock music as the most popular music genre in the United States.

CHAPTER 2

Teaching Self-Love

Building your Kings and Queens up early so nobody can tear them down

In 2016, Emory University in Atlanta introduced a course called "The Power of Black Self-Love." The objective of the course, designed for college students, is to bring awareness to the power of self-love in our society. As part of their final research projects, students were expected to highlight how Black self-love could bring about positive change in a racist society.

Countless research over the years has shown that by age five, kids are aware of race. Teaching our Kings and Queens self-love and pride in their skin color before they enter Kindergarten is crucial.

A few years ago, I watched a documentary about children's racial biases.[1] The study consisted of testing over one hundred kids from different backgrounds in the United States, from two age groups—four to five and nine to ten.

The kids were asked to pick across five different skin colors from dark to light, which kid was the bad kid, which kid they wanted to be friends with, and which skin color they would rather be.

It was disturbing to see that no matter the child's color and age, more than half of the kids picked the dark skin color child as the "bad child." They also picked the White child as whom they would want as a friend. Also, most of the Black kids appeared to show a positive bias toward lighter skin color and even more so toward White people.

As a mother of young Black children, it was heartbreaking to see how early kids formed opinions about race—most likely due to inherited trauma from past discrimination and racism.

For hundreds of years, we have suffered discrimination due to the color of our skin. It was pushed upon us that Black skin was inferior. To this day, we still deal with prejudice because of our skin color. It is only normal that we continue to suffer from the consequences of what we were taught for so many years. Some of our Black brothers and sisters have not yet realized that Black is beautiful. Some Black people still feel inferior and practice self-hate, sometimes unconsciously.

We need to acknowledge the weight of the past when raising our Black children. We should be kind to ourselves and practice self-love so we can teach our kids by example. We need to instill in our Kings and Queens a sense of pride in their early years, so they do not believe the lies people tell to this day about brown skin.

It is necessary to have these conversations with our young children about race and prepare them for the world. However, as we help build our kids' self-love, we also need to teach them that every skin color is beautiful. We should encourage them not to judge people by their skin color, but by their actions and character.

It is important to teach our kids, when they start noticing color, that they should embrace their skin and their features. We have to be proactive when it comes to the racism awaiting our children.

I am a mother of three young girls aged six and under. Since they were babies, I have tried to instill in them that they are beautiful inside out. I always remind my kids that they are smart and kind, and have beautiful internal and external features. I build their confidence up so that no one can tear it down. When I do my daughters' hair, I tell them how beautiful their hair is. Their father compliments them about their smarts and beauty as well. We also make sure to surround them with images of strong and beautiful Black women in all shapes and sizes.

If we spend time building our kids' confidence when they are young, they will go through childhood and into their teenage years with a high level of self-worth.

When you know your worth, nothing can be said to make you feel less valuable than you know you are.

In our family, our daughters have affirmations that they proudly say every day.

This habit helps build confidence. Time and time again, highly successful people have voiced how positive affirmations and speaking things into existence played a role in their success. The objective is for our Kings and Queens to repeat the daily affirmations so that they believe them, and they become undeniable truths for them. The statements should help them build confidence in themselves and in their abilities.

> I am a beautiful Black girl
> I am strong
> I am brave
> I am smart
> I am loved
> I am significant
> I matter
> I am enough
> I trust myself because I am a shero.

The girls are excited to say these words, and I am confident that it will help in the long run. As they grow, we will naturally make changes to the affirmations.

You can develop statements for your kids based on their age, gender, personality, interests. As they evolve, you can help them adjust their affirmations. The goal is to develop the habit of saying positive affirmations consistently. This practice will help our Kings and Queens believe great things about themselves and develop a positive attitude that will attract more positivity in their life.

At four years old, another four-year-old kid told my nephew that he would end up dead or in jail. That day, his parents had to have a difficult conversation with him about racism. They also realized that it was time to prepare my nephew for the racism he would face in the world, as this would most likely not be an isolated incident.

Not too long ago, we took our kids to the Martin Luther King Jr. Museum. My three-year-old twins, Aya and Kuimi, were not paying much attention. Still, it was an excellent experience for our then five-year-old daughter, Cecilia. I was dreading the conversation because she had not yet experienced racism. However, she was very aware of the fact that she was Black. My husband and I had already been working for years on encouraging her to be proud of her skin color. She was very sad when she heard about the challenges Black people faced but it was an enriching experience. She was proud to see that Martin Luther King Jr. was a Black man who had fought for equality for all.

As Cecilia wanted to play with kids at her school, she was told by three older boys that she could not because she looked like "poop." My then five-year-old daughter told the kids that their comment was inappropriate. At that point, the three elementary-aged kids realized they could get in trouble and told her that they would kill both her parents if she told anyone what they had said.

Shortly after, Cecilia told my husband and me what happened at school. I am still shocked that seven-year-old kids can use this type of language. However, that is the reality of the world. I was impressed by the fact that, as a five-year-old girl experiencing racism for the first time, she automatically understood what those three boys were doing and did not even cry. Cecilia said she was afraid of the boys. But the word used to describe her skin did not affect how she sees herself—because she is proud of her skin color. She told us about the threats those kids made, and my husband and I were able to take action at school. I believe that things would have been different if we had not been doing the work of helping build confidence about herself and her heritage.

Your hair is your crown.

One of the Black features attacked continuously over the years is our hair. I believe a woman has the right to decide what to do with her hair, whether it is to wear it natural, relax it, cut it, add to it, or dye it. However, when kids are young, I believe in teaching them to love their natural hair just the way it is. Kids can experiment with their hair at an age you as a parent deem appropriate. But, before adding to their natural beauty, they should learn to love the raw and uncut version of themselves.

I went to predominantly White schools throughout my life. I started relaxing my hair in middle school—this was after convincing the hairstylist to relax my hair without checking with my mother. I continued to wear my hair relaxed on and off until my mid-twenties.

I do not think we should have a say-so regarding what a woman chooses to do with her hair. What I believe is essential before you get to the point where you add to your natural beauty is to learn to love yourself the way you are.

At the time, I did not think much of my decision to relax my hair. It was not until years later that I realized that, given my age at the time, I did not make that decision for myself. The decision was made for me by society as a way to blend in a predominantly White school.

It was then that I realized I wanted to set a different expectation for my kids. I stopped using a relaxer on my hair from the moment I realized I was pregnant with my first child.

Wearing natural hair demands more effort—but when I think of the impact of me wearing my hair natural can have on my three young girls, and how they define beauty, I come to the conclusion that it is worth the extra effort.

If you tell a child every day from the time they are babies that their hair is beautiful and teach them to embrace it, it will have a lifelong impact on their self-love.

As parents, we have to remind ourselves that self-love is a constant practice. It is something we need to continue to do for ourselves and continue to teach our Kings and Queens as they grow up, especially during adolescence.

CHAPTER 3
Teaching Gratitude and Positive Thinking

Coaching children to appreciate what they have, and to embrace positivity

I am a firm believer in the power of gratitude. Practicing gratitude is choosing to focus on what you have instead of what you think you need. It is choosing to appreciate life for what it is today. When you spend time focusing on the good in your life, you keep an open heart, which leaves room for more blessings to come your way.

A 2013 study of Black youth between the ages of twelve and fourteen identified a positive relationship between gratitude and positive youth development.[1] According to the study, greater gratitude led to more abstinence from risky behaviors such as drug, alcohol use, and/or sexual intimacy, and higher academic and activity engagement.

We should teach our kids to approach life from a place of gratitude. As you learn to be more grateful for what you have in life, you become more aligned with what makes you happy. You then ask yourself the right questions and start dreaming about what would bring you even more happiness.

Gratitude helps you focus on the positive instead of the negative. As human beings, we can easily take things for granted—until we realize how much of a blessing they are and that we could lose them instantly. If you can read this book, you are blessed to see or hear, which many people cannot do. Most of us will find reasons to be grateful if we take the time to look inward.

A critical daily family tradition in our household is to express gratitude together every day. Every night, at the dinner table, each member of our family of five shares at least three things that they are grateful for about the day.

We started including our youngest, Aya and Kuimi, in the dinner tradition when they were two and a half years old. When asked what they were grateful for, they would always respond by repeating some of the things their older sister, my husband, or I mentioned in our thankfulness. When they were around three years old, Aya and Kuimi started understanding the exercise. At dinner time, they are now eager to share the parts of their day that brought them joy.

This practice is a valuable bonding time for us as a family, as we learn about the things that brought each other joy during the day. It is an even more important practice for our kids, who are learning to be thankful for experiences and things that they might have otherwise taken for granted.

When you keep track of what you are grateful for, it pushes you to be more present. You learn to look for moments of gratefulness throughout your day.

This gratitude practice has been working for our family. There are, of course, other ways to teach gratitude to children, such as keeping a gratitude journal. I encourage you to use our family tradition or find one that works best for your family.

Gratitude is an important element of positive thinking.

Positive thinking is one of the best gifts you can give your children. It fosters an environment where they can dream. It encourages them to believe in themselves before anyone else does and to go after their dreams.

I am a firm believer that our thoughts materialize. If you tell yourself every day that you are limited by what you can see and your circumstances, you will not get out of your current situation.

The word "cannot" is a trigger for me. I avoid using the word as I believe it prepares your mind for failure. If I hear my kids say they cannot do something, I automatically correct them and tell them that they can do anything as long as they work hard. I trust that if I keep repeating those words to them, it will plant the seeds to start believing that no mountain is too high to climb.

The other day, my three-year-old daughter Aya was trying to ride her bike. She was getting frustrated because she could not get it to start moving. She said, "Mommy, I cannot." Before I could respond, I heard my daughter Cecilia tell her that she could do anything she put her mind to. Aya decided to give it another try and succeeded. She had a big smile on her face. As she rode her bike in the backyard, she said to me, "Mommy, I did it." Though Cecilia might not yet understand the impact of the words she said to her younger sister, it shows me that she has been paying attention.

Over the years, I learned that practicing gratitude in difficult times is even more critical. Like many people, I have gone through my fair share of trials and tribulations. I have seen sadness on people's faces and heard it in their voices during those trying times.

What I realized is that dwelling on the negative aspects of my life was not a healthy alternative. Focusing on the positive elements in my life, such as faith and other blessings I have, is what continues to get me through during difficult times.

We need to encourage our children to practice gratitude and positive thinking. It will inspire them to believe that they can transcend any situation. It will motivate them to work hard and keep their mind focused on their objectives. Our kids should be encouraged to believe that if they work hard and continue to put their positive intentions into the universe, they will eventually reach their goals and aspirations.

The mind is a powerful thing. It can be our greatest ally and help us reach our wildest dreams, or it can stop us from doing so.

After earning my M.B.A., I joined a "Big Four"[*] accounting firm and obtained my Certified Public Accountant certification.

I was very grateful for the coveted experience, but after a few years, I started to feel the need to make a career shift to be more in alignment with the long-term vision I had for my life. I started thinking about writing a book, but I was not ready to take that step then. I put that dream on the backburner while exploring other career opportunities and looking for fulfillment in a more traditional career path.

I grew up in an environment where there were only a few career paths that were considered viable. Your major in college is what you are expected to do for the rest of your life. I believe that way of thinking is too restrictive. It took me years to realize that maybe I needed to take a chance and look outside the apparent fields in line with my educational and professional background.

I wanted to emphasize to my daughters the importance of being independent, secure, and going after their dreams. I also realized that I would not be able to live with

---

[*] "Big Four" is the nickname used to refer to the four largest professional services firms in the world: Deloitte, PricewaterhouseCoopers, Ernst & Young, and KPMG.

myself if I did not go after the new dreams I had for myself. I needed to walk the talk and bet on myself.

We should encourage our kids to dream big and be brave enough to take the road less traveled. Our children should grow up believing they can do anything they put their minds to as long as they give it their best shot.

CHAPTER 4
Teaching Solid Financial Habits Early

Teaching young kids the key fundamentals of money

In today's society, many adults struggle to save money and prepare for unexpected expenses.

In the United States, 37 percent of adults do not have the cash to face an unplanned 400-dollar expense, according to a report published by the Federal Reserve System's Board of Governors in May 2020.[1] They would have to borrow the money or sell something of value to face that expense.

Parents often receive money from family members for their kids' birthdays, Christmas, or other events. As a parent, you could put the money in a money market account and open a youth bank account with your child when they reach age five. This decision could help teach them a valuable lesson about money and saving.

Many Credit Unions have youth accounts for kids under age eighteen. These accounts typically come with higher interest rates than a regular savings account, at least for the first 1,000 dollars.

We opened a youth savings account at a Credit Union for our daughter Cecilia. On her fifth birthday, we took her to the bank to deposit money she had received over the first five years of her life. Once a quarter, we take Cecilia to the Credit Union, where she has her youth savings account. Every three months, before making a deposit, she sees the interest she has earned since her last visit and how much her balance has grown.

Every visit, she is reminded that leaving money in her high-yield savings account generates interest and helps her money grow.

You can do something similar with your kid to teach them about the time value of money.*

The most important lesson your child can learn with this exercise is that with time and compounded interest—money grows. Understanding compound interest by the time they turn eighteen will encourage them to save and help them make wiser decisions about their money. It will help them realize that money saved today will be worth exponentially more in the future.

From a very early age, kids should learn the three fundamental aspects of financial security: saving, spending, and giving back.

One of my favorite financial gurus, Suze Orman, likes to say that "the power of money is to make you feel secure." Understanding the three fundamentals aspects of money early will tremendously help kids in their pursuit of financial security.

In our household, we use a three-legged jar, which we started when our oldest child Cecilia turned five years old. When we started, Cecilia was responsible for doing two chores around the house five days a week to earn up to five dollars a week. We used five dollars, but the amount can vary based on what you are comfortable with as a parent. In our family, we planned to increase responsibility and income for every birthday. However, our now six-year-old daughter is aware that every year we expect her to ask for a raise and highlight her experience when negotiating a raise.

This practice teaches her the value of hard work and negotiation. It also familiarizes her with the idea that when you do not do your job, you can lose a significant portion of your income. Every week, Cecilia puts her hard-earned money in her jars. She can put up to 60 percent of her income in her spend jar. She also puts at least 10 percent in her share jar to give away, and 20 to 30 percent in her save pot every week. Some weeks, Cecilia chooses to put more in the give jar and thus less in the spend or save jar. However, she knows that her spending percentage should always be under 60 percent. When she receives monetary gifts or additional income for helping around the house, she also sets money aside to save and give. Cecilia decides how much of her money to give at a time. She enjoys donating to different causes and putting her money in the collection basket at church.

---

* The concept that money available today will be worth a lot more in the future.

I have been amazed at the ease and pleasure she has developed to give to less fortunate people and causes for which she has an interest. During the COVID-19 pandemic, she felt joy in making several donations to help people less fortunate than her to have access to food.

When we go shopping, she has the option to spend her money to buy something that she is interested in; but we noticed that she started paying more attention to prices in stores. I have noticed that Cecilia is more appreciative of what she has. She also does not seem to want nearly as much as other kids of her age. I remember when we used to go to the store, and she would always ask us if we could buy something for her. Trips to the store now provide an opportunity to talk to Cecilia about her wants as opposed to her needs. At six years old, she is starting to understand the importance of assessing a purchase and not buying everything you can afford. Cecilia also understands that for every dollar you earn, you should always think about saving and giving.

Another tradition that we have in our family is encouraging our daughters to give away at least as many new toys as they received for birthdays and Christmas. During birthdays and around Christmas, our girls go through their toys and select the ones that they will give away to less fortunate children. This tradition is another way that we teach our girls the importance of giving.

When our twin girls Aya and Kuimi turn four years old, we plan to introduce them to the concepts of having responsibilities and opportunities to earn income. At five, we will start discussing and implementing the three-legged jars to begin Aya and Kuimi's training on the three aspects of financial security: spending, saving, and giving back. We also plan to educate them on compound interest as we have been doing and will continue to do with Cecilia.

Teaching kids the importance of earning money, saving, and giving at a young age helps them understand the value of money. They start thinking about what they can afford to buy and whether or not the purchase makes sense. It also helps them understand the positive impact that giving money can have on others and that saving can have on their future.

Once your children understand the value of money, you can introduce them to the stock market by purchasing company shares through gift cards for instance. Several companies offer the option to buy fractional shares of stocks for as little as ten dollars. The objective is to introduce young people to the idea that they can own shares of companies they like. It will spike their interest in investing and encourage them to switch their focus from consumership to ownership.

Over the past year or so, I have been talking to Makayla, whom I consider like a niece, about the benefits of starting to invest a little bit of money every month in the stock market before she turns twenty-five.

As most twenty-two-year-olds, Makayla has not yet realized the value of starting to invest early. Recently, I gifted Makayla with gift cards redeemable for stock as a graduation present. It was not a glamorous gift, but I hope that it will lead to more interest on her part about the stock market.

At this time, our kids are too young to understand what such a gift represents. However, in a couple of years, we plan to have them select companies that they like and use that to help them identify which ones would be a good stock to purchase. As we do not want to overwhelm our young children with too much information, we view this as a symbolic practice. It is to spike interest in ownership and the stock market, more so that an investment that we expect to generate incredible financial returns. As mentioned, you can begin this practice with your kids with an investment as little as ten dollars. If the money available does not allow you to buy full shares, you should consider purchasing fractional shares.

These financial habits not only teach kids about saving and giving back but it also teaches them about investing, managing money, and the power of compound interest.

Sticking to these practices throughout your kids' early years and adolescent years will help them develop a healthy relationship with money by the time they are in high school.

Most kids enter adulthood with very little financial education. As a result, they make financial mistakes that they could have avoided if they had a healthier relationship and understanding of money.

As parents, we can educate our kids to avoid the typical financial traps most young adults fall into. Avoiding those traps will give our Kings and Queens a leg up. They will spend their late twenties/early thirties building their financial future without worrying about recovering from past financial mistakes like most young adults usually do.

CHAPTER 5
Assessing Your Financial Health

Taking a snapshot of your financial situation

Net worth
As parents with a desire to raise strong and financially secure kids, we should take the necessary steps to be financially secure ourselves in order to lead by example. Children will remember what their parents showed them more than what they told them.

The first step on the road to financial security is to take a snapshot of your financial situation. It helps you determine the challenges you have to overcome to reach your destination. For that reason, it is necessary to calculate your net worth. Your net worth is the value of the things you own that have monetary value (assets) minus everything you owe (liabilities).

Assets:
Money in your checking, savings, CDs or money market accounts
Real estate market value
Car market value (Kelley blue book)
Investment accounts value
Any other items of value you own.

Liabilities:
Mortgages' remaining balances
Student loans
Credit card debt
Car loans
Personal loans
Outstanding bills
Back taxes
Liens, judgments.

When you do not take the time to review all of your assets and liabilities, it is challenging to have a clear vision of your financials.

People tend to overestimate or underestimate their financial position.

Calculating your net worth is the best way to determine your financial health. It gives you a clear idea of where you are, which is your starting point toward building long-term wealth. If you find out that your net worth is in line with what you had in mind after going through this exercise, that is a great place to continue building wealth. You can continue to focus on saving and investing. You should regularly monitor your net worth to ensure that you stay on track with your savings and retirement goals. Calculating your net worth is the best way to determine your financial health.

An Excel spreadsheet is all that you need to keep track of your net worth. There are also free applications such as Personal Capital and You Need a Budget (YNAB) that you can use. These tools will help you track your net worth and all of your financial accounts.

After calculating your net worth, you may realize that you are not doing as well financially as you thought. Sometimes, even high earners find out that they have a negative net worth. The negative net worth could be due to spending habits or an excessive amount of debt.

If you have a negative net worth because you spend more than you make, this is an easy adjustment. You can go to the next chapter of the book, where I discuss income management.

If you have a negative net worth because of how much debt you have, do not be discouraged.

Now that you have the information—use it as motivation to work diligently at paying off debt so you can increase your net worth. The more debt you pay, the higher your net worth will be. In our society, it is normal to be comfortable with debt. Yet, when you have a financial liability, you have to pay someone else before you pay yourself. That can prevent you from investing in yourself.

Debt is like invisible handcuffs in the way of your freedom. But debt is not a death sentence. You can get out of debt by taking the steps mentioned in the book's debt management section. Do not dwell on past financial mistakes; what matters is the actions you take going forward.

There are many stories of people at various income levels who were able to turn their financial life around from a negative net worth to positive net worth. If you need inspiration and discipline, I recommend researching people from the Black community who have tackled the task of aggressively paying off debt who are now sharing their experiences with the world. Kiersten and Julien Sanders are a couple based in Atlanta who paid off 200,000 dollars of debt in five years. They started a blog called "Rich and Regular" to document their journey to financial independence. Talaat and Tai McNeely are a Black couple based in Chicago who paid off their twenty-five-year 300,000-dollar mortgage in five years. They are now financial educators and hosts of "The His and Hers Money Show." These are just a few examples of people who can inspire you in your journey to financial security.

Credit Score

In the United States, the credit score (FICO score) is used by lenders to track your habits when it comes to repaying money that you borrowed.

It is a three-digit number between 300 (poor) and 850 (excellent). There are three major national credit bureaus (Experian, Equifax, and TransUnion) that keep track of consumers' credit history and assign a credit score. Your credit score is used to determine the rate at which you will be able to borrow money. You should aim to have good credit with each bureau—a score higher than 750 to get the best interest rates to borrow money.

It is essential to check your credit score at least annually. You can also get a free credit report once a year. Getting in the habit of checking your report at least once a year will allow you to ensure that any activity reported on your report is accurate. It is also worth considering services to help you monitor, freeze, or lock your credit to reduce credit fraud exposure.

If you have a lower credit score due to prior financial mistakes or being taken advantage of, you should not be discouraged. Make it your mission to work on improving your score. You do not have to pay to increase your credit score. Some of the companies that specialize in helping people increase their credit score sometimes have questionable practices. If you decide you would like to hire someone to clean your credit, you should follow their actions carefully. It will help ensure they do not take any measures to increase your credit score that could hurt you in the long run.

CHAPTER 6
Optimizing Your Credit Strategy

Using credit to your advantage

An important tool for wealth building is credit. However, you have to understand how credit works to use it to your advantage.

Five key factors affect your credit score: payment history, credit utilization ratio, credit history, new credit inquiries, and mix of credit accounts.

Payment history accounts for about 35 percent of your credit history. It tracks how good your record is at paying your bills. The best way to keep track of your bills is to pay off the full balance every month. Paying off your credit card balance every month helps ensure that you do not pay interest charges.

The number one rule is always to pay your bills on time. If, for some reason, you cannot afford to pay the full balance at the end of the cycle, you should at least pay the minimum balance to avoid the negative impact on your credit. One single late payment could considerably affect your credit score.

If you ever end up in a situation where you know you will not be able to make a payment on time, you should be proactive. You should contact your creditor in advance and see if they are willing to work with you and give you more time to make the payment.

If you missed a payment and it is reported on your credit card statement, you should make the payment and see if your creditor will get the late fee removed as a courtesy.

The two habits that have helped me over the years are setting some time on my calendar once a week to review my credit card transactions, and making sure that my credit card bill is paid in full every month.

This habit has allowed me to pay my credit card bills on time every month. During my review, I usually schedule my payment two days before the due date. In case there is a technical difficulty, and the payment does not successfully go through, this would give me two extra days to ensure that my balance gets paid off on time.

I have never paid a cent in credit card interest since I opened my first credit card account fifteen years ago. However, I have received many rewards in the form of cashback and miles, thanks to my credit card utilization.

Sometime last year, I accidentally submitted my payment two days late and owed interest. I called my credit card company and asked if they could remove the interest charge. Given that it was the first time in fifteen years that I had ever submitted a late payment, as a courtesy, my credit card company agreed to remove the late fee.

You should use credit cards to maximize the rewards you can get without paying anything in return. As such, I encourage you to only charge your credit card for items you know you can afford to pay at the end of the cycle. You should also aim to set up a time every month to review your credit activity and pay bills.

Paying your bills on time and maintaining your credit balance pave the way to building a solid payment history. It might not always be attainable, but that is what you should strive for. It is the best way to ensure you have a stellar payment history.

Credit utilization, which accounts for 30 percent of your credit score, compares the amount of debt you owe to creditors to the amount of debt extended to you.

The two examples below illustrate the credit utilization ratio.

	Scenario 1	**Scenario 2**
Credit card debt	$4,000	$500
Credit limit	$0,000	$10,000
Credit utilization ratio	40%	5%

In the first scenario, person number one has a 10,000-dollar credit limit and 4,000 dollars in credit card debt. Her credit utilization ratio is 40 percent.

In the second scenario, person number two has a 10,000-dollar credit limit and 500 dollars in credit card debt. Her credit utilization ratio is 5 percent.

Person number two seems to be less reliant on credit. Based on credit utilization alone, she would have a higher credit score.

When you have a lower credit utilization ratio, you appear to be a lower risk to creditors.

Aim to have credit limits as high as you can, and use a small fraction of the credit available to you to optimize your credit score.

Usually, when I use my credit card for large purchases, I log in a couple of days later to pay off the balance.

An unwritten rule to optimize your credit utilization ratio is that you should not use more than 10 percent of any of your credit card accounts and your total credit limit. If you have monthly expenses that would exceed the 10 percent, what you can do is pay off the credit card balance whenever you reach the 10 percent threshold. That will allow you to maximize your credit rewards without negatively impacting your credit utilization ratio.

Credit history is the age of your credit accounts—it makes up 15 percent of your credit score. Your oldest account and the average age of all your accounts is what creditors are interested in.

The older accounts you have, the better your credit history will be. For that reason, you should be careful about closing old accounts as it can negatively impact your credit score.

There is not much a person can do to optimize credit history other than prioritizing having long-term credit accounts over new accounts.

Companies make credit inquiries when looking at your credit. Credit inquiries make up 10 percent of your credit score.

There are soft credit inquiries and hard credit inquiries. A soft inquiry is when you view your credit score or when a company pulls your credit without you applying for a new loan. A soft inquiry does not impact your credit score.

Your application for credit initiates a hard inquiry. This type of credit inquiries can negatively impact your credit score. The more hard inquiries you authorize, the more lenders will be inclined to think that you may need credit because you are in a difficult financial situation. Be conservative and limit your hard credit inquiries.

Two main types of accounts make up the credit mix: installment credit and revolving credit.

Installment debt has a specific end-date, as well as a fixed dollar amount due every month. Mortgage, student loans, and car debt are the most common examples of installment credit.

With revolving credit, there is no set amount due every month, as well as no end-date. Credit cards are the main types of revolving credit.

To optimize your credit score, you should aim to have a mix of both types of accounts. However, you should be conservative and limit how often you apply for new credit, and how many accounts you open.

Other factors that can affect your credit score

Outside of the main elements mentioned that can impact your credit score, other factors can potentially hurt your credit score. It is important to monitor your credit diligently.

Errors can sometimes appear on your credit score. It is crucial to take advantage of your free credit report and review your credit activity at least once a year. You are entitled to a free copy of your credit report from the three credit bureaus once a year. If you find an error on your report, you should report it to the three bureaus.

It is important to note that not paying your utility bills, medical bills, or rent on time can negatively impact your credit score. Though one late payment is unlikely to affect your credit score, unpaid invoices can cause your service providers to turn your debt over to a collection agency. Once the debt is sold to a collection agency, the debt collector can report the account to the credit bureaus. Also, in recent years, some landlords have started reporting rental payment data to the credit bureaus directly.

Delinquent child support, unpaid taxes, and parking tickets are other things that can affect your credit score.

It is essential to be responsible with your bills, minimize debt, and pay your creditors on time to have a good credit score. Having a high credit score gives you better borrowing rates and more financing options. We should teach our children about credit to help them understand what credit can do for them and to help them avoid mistakes that would hurt their credit.

Helping kids build credit history early

It takes approximately six months of credit history to create your first credit score. Most people will begin their credit journey with a score of around 500.

I started my journey as a young adult without any credit history. I could not qualify for any credit, so my older sister co-signed for my first apartment in college. I knew very little about credit, but I quickly realized that I needed to figure it out. I signed up for my first credit card fifteen years ago. Though I was very responsible with my bills, it took me years to get good credit, and even longer to have excellent credit.

I graduated from college during the great recession, when real estate prices were extremely low. After starting my first job, I wanted to buy a property. Unfortunately, due to my minimal credit history, I could not get a loan at a reasonable interest rate. As a result, I decided to wait a few years before investing in real estate. By then, prices were significantly higher.

I encourage you to be proactive and start your kids' credit education early. When they have a good understanding of money, spending, and savings, you can introduce concepts such as debit and credit cards.

Debit cards

Sometime around age ten, if your child already has solid money habits, you should consider obtaining a debit card for them. Several financial institutions allow parents to sign up for their minor children to have a debit card. The two advantages of minor debit cards are that parents can set spending limits and have access to their child's banking activity. Every month, you can sit down with your child to review the transactions, discuss their spending habits, and encourage them to continue to develop healthy financial habits. With those actions, you will teach them the importance of keeping a close eye on their finances and spending within their means. Allowing your children to have a debit card when they are ready is an excellent opportunity to further educate them on money management.

You can keep the card until you feel that your child is prepared to be responsible for it. However, you should continue to monitor your children's spending and review their transactions with them.

Credit cards

Most young adults enter college unaware of credit cards. Between the ages of thirteen and sixteen, most kids are ready to learn about credit cards. Typically, kids who manage their debit cards and income well and meet deadlines should be prepared to learn about credit cards.

We should teach our kids about credit score and credit cards and the importance of monitoring their credit.

Identity theft is an issue that we should all keep in mind. A few years ago, one of the major credit bureaus announced that they had a data breach that exposed the personal information of one hundred and forty-seven million people. The hackers accessed people's names, social security numbers, addresses, birth dates, and driver's license numbers. I encourage you to check if you or your children have been affected by the data breach. If you find that your personal information was exposed, you should consider getting a credit freeze or credit lock. It will ensure that you get notified any time someone tries to access your credit. If the data breach has not impacted you, you can still invest in a credit monitoring tool or review the information on your credit report once a year to ensure that it is accurate. These are habits you should teach your young adults—to minimize the risk of their credit being affected by identity theft.

When you introduce the concept of credit cards to your children, it is important to make it clear to them that with a debit card, you use money that you have in your bank account to pay for a transaction, while with a credit card you use borrowed money. They should know to only use credit cards when they have the cash to pay for a purchase.

We should teach our kids that credit cards and borrowing money, in general, come at a cost, which is interest. They should avoid paying interest by paying off their balance every month.

You can begin building your kids' credit early by adding them as an authorized user on your credit card by age sixteen. You do not have to give them the card until you think they are ready. However, by adding your children to your credit card as an authorized user, and by responsibly paying your bills, you would help establish your children's credit history.

The longer and healthier the credit history, the higher their score will be, and the better credit offers they will have if they decide to get a mortgage loan in the future, for example.

When your kids are ready and fully understand how credit works, you can allow them to keep the card. They should commit to only using the card for items they can pay for in cash, and pay off the balance every month. By age eighteen, the goal is that your children have good credit and know how to maintain it. It will provide additional opportunities to discuss financial responsibility with your children. Observing first-hand how you pay off the credit card bill every month will have a long-term impact on how they view credit cards. It will signal to them that they are not supposed to pay interest or carry a credit card balance.

Credit card rewards

Good credit cards provide perks, such as cashback, discounts, miles, or points that the cardholder can use for travel, restaurants, or even to purchase gift cards. When a person uses credit cards wisely, it benefits not only the card company but also the cardholder.

Every time your swipe your card, credit card companies get paid a percentage of the transaction. As a customer, you should also receive rewards from the credit card company for that transaction. That is a mutually beneficial relationship.

When you pay interest on your credit card, the relationship is advantageous to the credit card company but detrimental to your financial health. Because we want to avoid such a relationship with our credit card companies, we should wait until our kids can manage their bank accounts responsibly to introduce them to credit cards. Once you are comfortable that your Kings and Queens are using their credit cards responsibly, you should consider introducing them to the concept of credit card rewards.

Once they go away to college or start their first job, they will be able to use the education they learned at home to optimize their reward strategy.

I started my credit card journey with a credit card without any annual fees. After a week of research, I was able to identify the card that would give me the most reward without paying fees. My objective was to build my credit and get cashback for my everyday purchases.

For years, I would swipe my card and pay off my balance at the end of my cycle. In exchange, I was happy to receive cashback to apply toward travel or other purchases.

A few years later, when airlines started charging for checked luggage, I signed up for my second credit card. I was traveling regularly and needed to find a way to avoid the fee. With that card, my first luggage is free, and so is my travel companion's first bag. The annual fee was 75 dollars, which I was not excited to pay. However, I quickly realized that as long as I took two trips per year, the card would pay for itself. I still use that card regularly now. It helps me earn points toward free travel every year, and it also allows me to earn miles toward airline status. You should consider that approach with your kids, starting with an annual fee-free card. As they become more comfortable down the line and their needs change, they can look into another card as long as the benefits outweigh the costs.

CHAPTER 7
Making the Most of Your Income

Learning to stretch your income

Budgeting

A handy tool to help you make the most of your income is budgeting. Budgeting is planning your expenses (most commonly for the month or the year) based on your income.

When I was a kid, my mother often told me how important it was to be content with what I had. When I started receiving a small allowance from my parents, she told me that I should always save at least 20 percent of my money. I believe that lesson motivated me to create my first budget on a piece of paper at the age of thirteen. My budget had very few line items, but it was sufficient to give me a clear idea of how much of my allowance I could spend. It was also a way to ensure that I met the minimum 20 percent savings requirement set by my mother. Ever since then, I have been using budgets to manage my finances.

Having expense targets is a proactive approach that helps you be intentional about your spending. It helps align how you spend your money with what is of importance to you.

If you do not have a monthly budget yet, the first step is to track your expenses. If this is not something you practice already, I encourage you to get started now and track your spending for a month.

Paying close attention to how you spend your money can be an eye-opening experience.

When I got my first job out of college, I used to go out a couple of times a week with friends to try out new restaurants in the city. At the end of the first two months, I realized how much that new habit was costing me. I had spent close to 800 dollars in two months. Had I continued with that habit for a year—that would have cost me 5,000 dollars a year. As a young college graduate, it did not seem like a good use of my money. As such, I needed to adjust. I continued to get together with my friends, even though the restaurant discovery adventures became a once to twice a month activity. At that time, I also paid attention to other expenses, like how much I spent shopping for clothes. I realized that though I was saving a reasonable amount of money, I wasted money on things that did not add much value to my life.

I challenge you to track your expenses for the next month. It will change your approach when it comes to how you spend your hard-earned dollars.

During this period, I encourage you to avoid using cash, as it makes it harder to keep track of expenses. Use your card so that you can, at the end of the cycle, quickly review your spending by category. If you have to use cash, write down the amount of the expense and its purpose right away.

After thirty days or so, you will be able to see where your money is going. As you review your monthly expenses, ask yourself if your spending habits are in line with what is important to you. Consider where to make adjustments, which expenses you want to prioritize, and how to increase your savings.

When you do not track your expenses, it is easy to spend money on things that will make you smile for a few days or even a couple of weeks. You want to make sure that you are spending your money on what matters to you.

Tracking your expenses will highlight your bad spending habits and help identify potential savings areas. It is a great baseline to build or modify your budget. A monthly financial plan will make you feel more in control of your finances and help you stay on track with your financial goals.

Once you have a good idea of your monthly expenses, you can begin working on your budget. Consider assigning every dollar to a specific category (including the saving category). This practice, called zero-based budgeting, helps you keep track of all the money you have.

As a general rule, most people know they should spend less than they earn. But, when you do not have a clear plan for your income, you can miss out on additional saving opportunities.

At the end of this chapter is a sample monthly budget.

We use different financial plans in my family for monthly and long-term planning, but our household's "maintenance budget" covers all of our recurring monthly expenses. It separates our expenses between twenty-three categories, including kid-related costs, food, gas, saving, entertainment.

I encourage you to use this tool as a baseline to customize your budget. It is essential to review your spending and compare it to your plan every month. If needed, you can make adjustments. The most important thing to remember is that you can only allocate the income that you have coming in.

Budgeting helps you manage your money more efficiently. It keeps you accountable for every dollar that you earn. It will also help align your spending with things and experiences that bring you joy. Reviewing your expenses every month and comparing them to the plan helps keep you on track.

Below is a list of free tools that can help with the budgeting process. These tools will help you track your spending and create and manage your budget(s), savings, and debt.

- You Need a Budget (YNAB)
- Mint
- Clarity Money
- EveryDollar
- GoodBudget
- Spendee

With most of these applications, you can streamline your finances by linking your financial accounts—such as bank accounts, credit cards, and investments—to the application. If you choose to do so, the application will automatically pull your financial information from those accounts and provide an overview of your finances. However, if you are not comfortable linking your account, you can also use Excel and Google Sheets for your budgeting needs.

Optimizing your tax savings

Optimizing your tax savings is an essential part of making the most of your income. There are a few steps that everyone can take to minimize their income tax liability.

1. Checking your tax withholding
It is critical to check the tax withholding on your paycheck. In the United States, the IRS provides a withholding calculator on its website to help estimate the right amount of withholding from your paycheck. Using the calculator can help you avoid overpaying or underpaying your taxes.

2. Reviewing your pre-tax benefits
In chapter ten of this book, we take a close look at retirement savings with pre-tax income. In addition to contributing to a retirement account with pre-tax dollars, there are other expenses that can help reduce your taxable income.

Health-related expenses

If you are an employee, you can elect to participate in your employer's health insurance plan if the option is available. Your health insurance premium expenses are deducted from your pre-tax income. Also, you can opt to participate in your company's flexible spending account or health savings accounts. Contributions to any of these two accounts will allow you to set aside pre-tax dollars for your medical expenses and reduce your tax liability.

Moreover, in 2020, any medical expenses higher than 10 percent of your adjusted gross income (AGI) can be deducted from your AGI. AGI represents your gross income minus any pre-tax deductions. Pre-tax deductions help lower your tax liability.

Dependent care deductions

As of 2020, the IRS allows families to contribute up to 5,000 dollars per year to care for children under age thirteen. Contributions are made through payroll deductions, which reduces your taxable income. Contributions are reimbursed to you as you incur the expenses.

Charitable contributions

Your charitable donations qualify for a tax deduction if made to a tax-exempt organization. For any contributions in cash or property of 250 dollars, the IRS requires a written acknowledgment from the charity.

Besides the most common pre-tax benefits mentioned above, you should look at other items that may lower your tax liability. A few expenses to consider are paying disability and life insurance premiums with pre-tax dollars. You should also explore other tax credits you may qualify for, such as income, savings, homeowner, education credits, and deductible interest. Keeping a good record of your business expenses is crucial as eligible business expenses will reduce your taxable income.

As you look to optimize your tax savings, consider itemizing your deductions if your tax-deductible items exceed the standard deduction.

Sample Monthly Budget*

Kids	24
College Savings	5
Mortgage	5
Property Taxes	2
House	6
Home Warranty	1
Phone Bill	1
Internet, TV	1
Utilities	2
Lawn + Pest + Mosquito	1
Personal Care	2
Groceries	5
Car Insurance	1
Cars	4
Other Insurance	1
Entertainment	2
Health	1
Travel	7
Other	3
Short Term Savings	3
Dream Savings	1
IRA Contributions	7
Other Long Term Savings	15
Total Expenses	100
After-tax Income	100
Difference	0

* Above is a sample budget for take-home pay only (after taxes and deductions). For that reason, pre-tax payroll deductions such as health savings' accounts, dependent care deductions are not included in this budget.

CHAPTER 8

Managing Debt

Understanding the fundamentals of debt

One of the critical steps toward a more secure financial life is to understand and adequately manage debt. When you are not educated about debt and its impact, you can put yourself in a bad financial situation that could take years to resolve.

There has been countless research showing discriminatory debt practices toward minorities. In 2019, the University of California, Berkley, released a study highlighting unfair practices in consumer lending.[1] According to the study, Black and Latino applicants tend to have higher interest rates than their White counterparts due to discriminatory lending practices.

The path to getting into debt is much easier than it should be. When facing difficult times, it can be tempting to resort to debt to solve an issue. However, you have to be very careful with the debt that you take on, as its long-term effect can be devastating.

Lauren, an acquaintance of mine in her early thirties, shared the amount of stress she was under due to debt. She had close to 125,000 dollars of student loans, car loans, and credit card debt. That was the first of several conservations we had about personal finance and debt management.

Lauren, a working professional with a master's degree, took on a lot of debt over the years, without fully understanding the consequences. She had about 100,000 dollars of student loan debt and 20,000 dollars remaining on her car loan. She also had 5,000 dollars of credit card debt. Lauren had deferred payment on her student loans for two years. At the time she opted to postpone her student loan repayment temporarily, she was not aware that interest would continue to accrue during that period. Over the two-year deferment, her student loan balance increased by about 10,000 dollars due to interest accrual.

Fast forward a few years, she was now thinking about purchasing a home. After several conversations, Lauren realized she could not afford to make that next step until she could get her finances in order. Lauren took a close look at her net worth and began to educate herself on personal finance for the first time. She decided to drastically reduce her living expenses to pay off her debt in five years. Lauren attempted to sell her car back to the dealership, but it turned out not to be a good alternative. She had upgraded her car a couple of years prior, and like many people, when Lauren shopped for the car, she focused on how much of a car payment she could fit in her budget, disregarding the total cost of the purchase.

Two years later, if she sold the car back, she would owe 4,000 dollars on the car loan after the sale due to the car's high-interest loan. Besides, she would need to spend a few more thousand dollars to pay cash for a reliable vehicle.

Instead, Lauren committed to continuing to pay the car loan. She also decided to allocate a significant portion of her income for the next five years to pay off her debt. Lauren chose to pay at least 30,000 dollars toward her debt every year. She also applied any bonus she received toward her debt. She wanted to be debt-free in five years, which would be around age thirty-seven.

Lauren finished graduate school and started working at age twenty-four. Due to her past financial mistakes, she lost more than ten years she could have spent building financial security. But, given the amount of debt Lauren was in her early thirties, the situation could have been much worse. Lauren ended up with significant debt due to her lack of personal finance education. However, she was making a pretty good income and did not have any dependents. Those two advantages gave her the luxury to rectify her mistakes and begin her financial independence journey around her mid-thirties.

As minority borrowers, we need to have a solid understanding of debt-related concepts and do the appropriate research before taking on any debt. There are still predatory lending practices toward minorities that we should protect ourselves from by being financially educated.

As parents, we must learn about debt, understand the difference between good and bad debt, and understand the impact of interest rates.

Interest rate

Interest is the cost a bank or lender will charge you to borrow money. Interest rates vary based on the type of loan you are requesting.

Consumer debt will typically carry a much higher interest rate than a mortgage or student loan debt.

Good debt versus bad debt

In the financial world, there is often a distinction between "good debt" and bad debt. Typically, good debt has the potential to go up in value or generate income for the borrower in the long run. If neither of the two applies, it is usually considered bad debt.

You should avoid bad debt or toxic debt at all costs. However, you should also limit the amount of good debt you take on. When used wisely, good debt can help you achieve long-term financial success; but too much of it can also get in the way of your financial security. In this chapter, we will examine both types of debt.

Good debt is debt that you take on expecting to receive positive financial returns in the long run (income or increase in value). The most common examples of good debt are mortgage debt and student loans. Some of the returns expected from good mortgage and student loan debt are property appreciation and income increase. However, you have to be cautious, because mortgage and student loan debt at steep interest rates do not qualify as good debt. Also, having too much unnecessary "good" debt can turn into bad debt. You have to be conservative in terms of how much "good debt" you take on. It is essential to research the going rates for the type of loan you are exploring. Before taking on any debt, you should request quotes from different lenders to ensure the rate at which you are borrowing money is reasonable.

Mortgage debt

Homeownership is part of the American dream. The purchase of a home in the United States usually involves borrowing money in the form of a mortgage, since most people cannot afford to pay for a house in cash. Agents, lenders, and other parties make a living helping their customers purchase a home. For that reason, they often encourage people to buy a home before they are ready, with very little money for the down payment.

Owning and maintaining a home is costly. It is wise to wait until you are prepared to face the cost of home ownership before purchasing a house.

It is possible to buy a house with very little money down (less than 5 percent for the down payment); however, it comes at a higher risk and cost of borrowing money.

It is crucial to practice due diligence before purchasing a home. This step can be the difference between your investment going up in value as opposed to losing value.

Conventional mortgage loans

A conventional mortgage loan is a mortgage that is not guaranteed or insured by a government agency. For conventional loans, putting less than a 20 percent down payment on a house will result in the lender requiring you to pay a monthly premium (private mortgage insurance: PMI). PMI is usually between 0.55 and 2.25 percent of the original loan amount each year. At those rates, the monthly premium on a 150,000 dollars mortgage would cost between 825 and 3,375 dollars extra per year. Some lenders advertise loans with less than 20 percent down without PMI. You should be aware that they usually come with a higher interest rate. In both instances, the cost of borrowing money will be higher since your down payment is below 20 percent.

If it makes sense to incur the PMI, consider putting at least a 10 percent down payment on your house to reduce long-term financial stress. It is a possibility that the real estate market will go down during the time of your homeownership. A 10 percent down payment or more will help avoid owing more on the house than what it is worth during the downturn.

FHA loans

An FHA loan is a mortgage loan backed by the Federal Housing Administration. First-time home buyers are often attracted to FHA loans due to the less stringent requirements in terms of down payment and credit scores. FHA loans require an upfront fee of about 1.75 percent of the loan amount and a monthly premium (mortgage insurance premium: MIP). The premium is added to your mortgage payment, usually between 0.45 and 1.05 percent of the loan. For a 150,000 dollars mortgage, the upfront fee would be 2,625 dollars and the MIP between 675 and 1,575 dollars per year.

Depending on your situation, FHA loans might be attractive; however, it is important to factor in the additional cost of FHA loans mentioned above.

If you are looking to purchase your home and get the house at a good deal (considerably below market value), it might make sense to put less money down.

Student loan debt
The cost of attending college continues to increase faster than inflation. Most Americans do not have the privilege to go to college on full-ride scholarships or have parents who can afford to pay the full cost of their college expenses. To get an education, the majority of college students have to take on student loans. Student loan debt is the second highest consumer debt in the United States of America, only behind mortgage debt. In the third quarter of 2019, the outstanding student loan debt in America was 1.5 trillion dollars.[II]

In the United States, millennials are the most indebted college students in history. Unfortunately, the average salary for millennials has not increased as fast as the cost of getting a college education.

According to the National Center for Education Statistics (NCES), Black students are more likely to take on debt (71 percent) than their White peers (56 percent).[III] The racial wealth gap between Black and White students is a key factor explaining the student loan debt disparity between Black and White students.

In 2016, Black college students with bachelor's degrees graduated on average with a student loan debt of 7,400 dollars higher than their White peers.[IV] Four years after graduation, the Black-White student loan debt gap is expected to grow to 25,000 dollars. Contributing to the growing gap are lower wages earned by Black graduates upon graduation (7,000 dollars annual difference with White graduates), interest accrual, and enrollment in graduate school, which allows repayment deferral.[IV]

Often, college students are encouraged to borrow as much money as they can without being educated on the impact that these student loans can have on their financial future.

In July 2019, the National Association for the Advancement of Colored People (NAACP) and the Center for Responsible Lending (CRL) co-wrote a report to address the burden of student loans on minorities and how it contributes to the widening wealth gap in America.[V]

Our kids should not get into excessive student loan debt as it will reduce their discretionary income until the debt is paid back. The key to avoiding this financial mistake is to educate our kids before they decide how much and which student debt to get.

For instance, as part of the federal direct loan program, you can qualify for a subsidized or an unsubsidized loan for undergraduate degrees. While subsidized loans will carry the same interest rate as an unsubsidized loan, the interest will not begin accruing while you are in college. Interest on unsubsidized loans begins accruing from the moment the money is disbursed to you. For that reason, if your child needs student loans to attend college and qualifies for subsidized loans, it should be their first choice. A subsidized loan will result in less interest owed over time.

Our kids should pick a major they are interested in; however, they should treat student loans as an investment in their future. As such, the investment should be analyzed to ensure that it generates appropriate returns. We should help our Kings and Queens research the average first-year salary for their major(s) of interest. Before taking on student loans, they should perform a cost-benefit analysis of their major.

As a rule of thumb, it is not a good idea to take on student loans that exceed the excepted salary upon graduation. The same applies to graduate school loans if they decide to attend graduate schools. Upon graduation, we should help keep our kids focused on aggressively working to pay off their student loans. Until they have paid off their student debt, they should avoid increasing their expenses when their incomes increase.

Tanya, an acquaintance of mine, took on 40,0000 dollars of student loans to pursue her undergraduate degree. The loan amount was reasonable based on her expected starting salary. When the time came to start paying her student loans, Tanya did not feel that she could afford to make the monthly payment. She decided to defer her payment until she would be able to get a better job. However, Tanya was a single mother who did not fully understand the intricacies of loan deferment. Five years later, Tanya began paying down her student loan balance. But she quickly refinanced and deferred the loan pay down again as she was going through financial troubles. Ten years later, Tanya's student loan balance is 100,000 dollars. Over the years, Tanya's decision to repetitively defer and refinance her initial 40,000 dollar loan cost her 60,000 dollars in ten years. Tanya's story should serve as a motivation to aggressively tackle student loan debt.

The following examples are a few scenarios of student loan pay down using Tanya's loan situation.

Scenario 1: Five-Year Payoff

Loan amount	$40,000
Interest rate	4.5%
Years to repay	5
Monthly payment	$746
Payment after five years	$44,760
Interest	$4,760

Scenario 2: Fifteen-Year Payoff

Loan amount	$40,000
Interest rate	4.5%
Years to repay	15
Monthly payment	$306
Payment after fifteen years	$55,080
Interest	$15,080

Scenario 3: Ten-Year Payoff after Ten-Year Deferral

Loan amount	$100,000
Interest rate	4.5%
Years to repay	10
Monthly payment	$1,036
Payment after five years	$124,320
Interest	$84,320[1*]

Paying off the 40,000 dollar loan in five years would result in paying close to 5,000 dollars in interest rate. But, stretching the payment over fifteen years would result in 15,000 dollars in interest. The third scenario reflects Tanya's student loan balance after ten years, after her decision to defer and refinance repayment on her student loans several times.

For the next ten years, Tanya will pay 24,320 dollars of interest and the additional 60,000 dollars accrued during the past ten years. Tanya will pay a total of 84,320 dollars in interest on a 40,000 dollar loan. To simplify the calculation, the irregular loan payments Tanya made in the past ten years are not included. Those payments would show an even higher interest paid by Tanya on the loan. A five-year plan to repay student loans seems like a reasonable sacrifice on the road to financial freedom. It will also help save a significant amount of interest that would otherwise be incurred if taking longer to repay a student loan.

Bad debt

Bad debt is borrowing money to make purchases that lose value or do not produce income.

The most common examples are credit cards, auto loans, and payday loans. Bad debt comes at very high interest rates compared to good debt. As a rule of thumb, we should teach our children to avoid bad debt by saving to make purchases that will not harm their financial position.

Credit card debt

Credit card debt occurs when a person makes a purchase using money borrowed from a credit card company. The cost to borrow is known as the annual percentage rate (APR). According to the Federal Reserve, that cost is very high, with the national average rate around 16.61 percent as of February 2020.[VI]

During challenging economic times, credit cards are often used by the Black community, which is more likely to pay higher interest rates.

Often, credit card holders pay the minimum amount to avoid having to pay late fees. As many people from our community are not educated on this subject, we fall into the trap and make the minimum payment, not knowing that it does not do much toward paying down the initial debt balance, and may adversely affect our credit score.

In 2019, the average credit card balance was 6,194 dollars according to Experian.

For American Express, the minimum credit card payment is the higher of 35 dollars or 1 percent of your balance plus fees and interest. In this case, paying off the 6,194 balance would take seventeen years and three months and result in interest of 13,480 dollars in addition to repaying the 6,194 dollar principal balance.

We need to educate ourselves and learn to use credit cards to our advantage. As a general rule—we should teach our children to limit the number of credit cards they have and to pay off their credit card balance every month. The objective is to avoid paying any interest.

If you do not pay off your credit card balance in full at the end of your cycle, the credit company will make even more money on your purchase. You will end up paying 15 to 19 percent interest on the transaction, which will make this relationship beneficial to only one party—the credit card company. When you use a credit card as a tool, you can earn rewards. Typically, the least attractive credit cards are store credit cards. We should discourage our kids from those types of cards as they only provide advantages if you shop at a specific store. Stores often offer significant discounts to sign up for a credit card to attract customers. However, the cost of adding another credit card to your credit history is not worth it.

You should educate yourself on credit cards and teach your children, so they know how to use them to their advantage.

Car financing

Car financing is the purchase of a car using an auto loan with an agreement to repay the loan over a specific term.

According to Experian PLC, one of the leading credit report firms, as of Q3 2019, the outstanding loan balances were 1.22 trillion dollars with average loan terms of 64.9 months and 69.3 months for used and new cars, respectively.[VII]

The average loan amount for a used car was 20,446 dollars and 32,480 dollars for a new car. The average interest rates on those loans were between 5.96 percent for new vehicles and 9.56 percent for used cars. The average monthly payment was 550 dollars for new cars and 393 dollars for used cars.

Below is an illustration of the financial impact of the average car loan on a person's finances.

New Car Loan		**Used Car Loan**	
Loan amount	$32,480	Loan amount	$20,446
Interest rate	5.96%	Interest rate	9.56%
Years to repay	5.8	Years to repay	5.4
Monthly payment	$550	Monthly payment	$393
Payment after term	$38,115	Payment after term	$25,506
Interest	$5,635	Interest	$5,060

Millions of Americans finance cars without truly understanding the impact of that decision on their financial future.

Cars, excluding collectible cars, are not investments. Cars can quickly lose more than 10 percent of their value shortly after being driven off the lot.

A new car usually loses 20 percent or more of its value in the first year, then another 10 percent every year after that for the next four years.[VIII] After the first five years, the average new car can be worth about 40 percent of its original price. The average new car, purchased for 32,480 dollars will likely be worth 12,292 dollars (40 percent) five years later.

That is the main reason why used vehicles are a great option, especially on the path to financial freedom. By purchasing a well-maintained used car with low mileage, you minimize the depreciation hit you would have incurred if you had purchased the car brand new.

Car loans are so accessible that it encourages people to switch cars more often than they need to. Consumers often mistakenly focus on the car payment amount when car shopping. As a result, they neglect the long-term impact that car financing will have on their finances.

We need to understand and teach our kids the power of saving to buy a car that they can afford. Usually, people saving to purchase a car in cash tend to select more afford-able cars and gain more freedom in return.

For instance, if you were to set aside 393 dollars (the amount of the average loan payment on a used car) every month, after twelve months, you would be able to buy a car in CASH for 4,716 dollars.

It will not be a fancy car, but there are reliable starter cars for that price. You can also choose to save for an extra year to get a nicer car. Most importantly, that sacrifice comes with freedom. You will not have to worry about your car payment every month. For the next fifty-two months which is the remainder of the average used car loan term (the average term is sixty-four months), you could split the 393 dollars every month in a savings account as follows:

52 Months Saving (no $393 car payment)

$193 savings a month for next car	$10,036
Save remaining $200 a month	$10,400

As evidenced by this table, after fifty-two months, you would have over 10,000 dollars in savings or emergency funds (excluding any interest earned). You would also have 10,000 dollars available for the next car purchase. The decision to buy the car you can afford today—and not spend tomorrow's money to buy a car—would help secure your financial future.

Payday loans

A payday loan or cash advance is a small amount of money (typically 500 dollars or less) that you can borrow at a high cost until payday. The average loan term is approximately two weeks to be repaid at 391 percent interest or more on average.

Payday loans are usually issued to borrowers with bad credit history who need the money to face an emergency. Approximately, twelve million Americans use payday loans every year.[ix]

While less than 4 percent of American adults use payday loans, it is essential to note that payday loans are more prevalent among the twenty-five to thirty-four age group. We should have discussions with our young adults about the importance of saving and the actual cost of cash advances. We should protect our children by teaching them that they should avoid payday loans at all costs.

Getting out of debt

People make bad financial decisions every day. It can be the result of a lack of financial education or a lack of understanding, but sometimes, it is the only choice a person has.

If you are struggling with debt management, you should not feel discouraged.

The first step to getting out of debt is to identify which debt to pay off aggressively.

Any liability with an interest rate of 7 percent or more is a high-interest debt. Any interest rate higher than 7 percent is likely to cost you more than the returns you would get from investing in an S&P 500 index fund in the stock market.

The S&P 500 is a stock market index tracking the performance of five hundred large-cap companies listed on the United States stock exchanges. Since 1957, the average annual return of the S&P 500 has been approximately 8 percent.

Categorizing debt between high-interest and low-interest categories is for reference purposes only. You should not invest money that you intend to use to pay down debt in the stock market, in the hopes of generating returns. Nobody can time the stock market, so it is wise to only invest money in the market that you will not need for the next ten years or more.

It is important to focus on paying off any bad debt aggressively because debt limits your freedom.

There are several options to tackle getting out of debt. The two most popular methods are the debt snowball and avalanche methods.

Debt snowball method

The debt snowball method involves paying off your debt, starting with the lowest balance regardless of the interest rate. Under this method, you make the minimum payments on each of your accounts and then allocate any extra money that you have toward paying off your smallest debt.

Once you have paid off the debt with the smallest balance, then you move on to the debt with the second lowest balance, until you finally tackle the debt with the largest balance.

Let us say, for example, that you have three accounts with the following balances:

> 7,000 dollars owed on your car loan at 9 percent interest rate with a 150 dollar minimum monthly payment.
> 4,000 dollars owed on your credit card at 18 percent interest rate with a 110 dollar minimum monthly payment.
> 5,000 dollars owed on a personal loan at 8 percent interest rate with a 185 dollar minimum monthly payment.

Under the debt snowball method, you make the minimum payment on all three account balances every month until paid off. You start aggressively paying off the credit card debt, which has the lowest balance. You continue to put any extra money that you have toward the credit card until you have paid off that balance. When the credit card is paid off, you then move on to the personal loan, which has the second smallest balance. Once you have paid off the balance on the personal loan, you can focus on paying off the car with the highest balance.

Debt avalanche method

The debt avalanche method or debt stacking method encourages to focus on the debt with the highest interest rate. You make the minimum payment on each of your debts and allocate any excess funds to pay down the debt with the highest interest rate aggressively. Once you have paid off that debt, you move on to the debt with the second-highest interest rate until you have paid that one off. You continue until you have paid off all of your debt.

Let us use the same example as we did under the debt-snowball method.

> 7,000 dollars owed on your car loan at 9 percent interest rate with a 150 dollar minimum monthly payment.
> 4,000 dollars owed on your credit card at 18 percent interest rate with a 110 dollar minimum monthly payment.
> 5,000 dollars owed on a personal loan at 8 percent interest rate with a 185 dollar minimum monthly payment.

Under the debt avalanche method, you make the minimum payments on all three accounts. You pay any extra money that you have every month toward the highest interest rate. In this case, it is the credit card debt—with an 18 percent interest rate. Once you have paid off the credit card, you pay off the car loan with the 9 percent interest rate. You continue to make the minimum payments on the personal loan, and then any extra money goes toward the car loan until you have paid off the car debt. Finally, you focus on your personal loan, which has the lowest interest rate.

There are advantages and disadvantages to each method. With the avalanche method, you would pay less in interest by focusing on the debt with the highest interest rate. You would also pay off your debt quicker. The disadvantage of the debt avalanche method is that it is harder to stay motivated. The focus is on the highest interest and not the lowest debt. It might take a while before you can pay off your first debt.

The most significant advantage of the debt snowball method is psychological because it keeps you motivated. As you focus on the smallest balance, you pay off your first debt, which motivates you to keep going. However, in the long run, it will cost you more than the avalanche method. It will also take you longer to pay off all your debt.

Choosing between the debt snowball or the avalanche method is a personal decision. It depends on whether it is more important to you to have external motivation to stay on track, or if it is more important to you to pay less interest and be out of debt quicker.

Other popular ways to work on paying off debt is balance transfer and debt consolidation.

Balance transfer

A balance transfer is when you move the balance on one of your credit cards to another card with a lower interest rate. Balance transfers typically come with a 0 percent introductory APR for a short period. During the introductory period, your payments will solely be applied toward your principal balance and not interest charges. A balance transfer is something you could consider if you have good credit, an account with high interest rate, and intend to pay off the loan faster. However, it only makes sense if the fees for transferring the balance are lower than what you would save in interests on the first card, and if the APR is lower. The example below illustrates when a balance transfer is a good alternative.

Scenario 1:
You owe 7,000 dollars to Bank A at 22 percent APR.
You were planning to pay off the debt in 24 months and incur 1,555 dollars in interest (approximately 356 dollars monthly payment).
Bank B sends you an offer of 0 percent APR for 18 months and 15 percent APR after 18 months.
Bank B charges a balance transfer fee $210 dollars (3 percent).
Bank B approves the balance transfer and pays your credit card balance to Bank A.
For 18 months, your 363 dollars payment will go toward paying down the principal balance only.
In 18 months, you will pay 6,534 dollars toward your 7,000 dollars balance without incurring interest. After the first 18 months, your remaining balance will be 466 dollars, and you will start paying the new APR on the debt, which is 15 percent instead of the initial 22 percent. With this balance transfer, you would be able to pay off the debt in 20 months instead of 24 months and save over 1,000 dollars in fees (after deducting the transfer fee of 210 dollars), representing 14 percent of the initial balance.

In this instance, if you know you can make the 363 dollars every month, it is worth transferring your balance under the conditions offered.

Debt consolidation

Another way to pay off your debt is to consolidate all of your debt under a personal loan—if you can get a personal loan at a lower interest rate than your current debt. You then have one balance and one monthly payment at a lower interest rate. It is a good alternative if you are able to secure a lower interest rate on your loan, and if the fees involved are lower than the money you would spend on interest charges. If there are not any fees, and the interest rate is lower, then it is a good alternative. But if you have to pay fees that will be higher than the interest charges, then it does not make sense to consider this alternative.

Student loans

According to data from the Pew Research Center in 2014, the median net worth of households headed by a college graduate under the age of forty, who had student loan debt, was 8,700 dollars.[x] On the other end, the median net worth of households headed by a college student under age forty but without student loan debt, was seven times higher, at 64,700 dollars.[xi]

Society views student loans as "good debt." However, student loan debt, like other debt, limits your saving and investing potential. It also restricts your ability to take a financial chance to pursue your passions or dreams. For instance, let us say you want to work with a nonprofit organization whose mission is close to your heart. But, the salary will not allow you to reimburse your student loans. Even if the position is aligned with your long-term goals, you would probably not be able to pursue that route. You would likely have to commit to the position that would pay you more, even if it did not fit your long-term strategy. When you owe debt, you have to prioritize paying someone else before considering investing in your dreams and aspirations.

Some people believe in making the minimum payment toward their student loan, betting on loan forgiveness.

There are a few conditions under which your student loan debt can be forgiven.

One way to get your student loans paid off is through the Public Service Loan Forgiveness (PSLF). Under the PSLF, if you make student loan payments under a qualifying repayment plan for ten years, the remaining balance of your student loans will be forgiven. It might be a good alternative if you are interested in a government career. However, you have to consider that it is a ten-year commitment minimum to pay your student loans to take advantage of that benefit.

Under the Teacher Loan Forgiveness Program, a highly qualified teacher can also get a portion of their debt forgiven—up to 17,500 dollars as of 2020.

Full-time members of the Peace Corps or AmeriCorps may also qualify for federal student loan forgiveness.

Another strategy that people often pick is to choose an income-driven plan and repay the loan until their student loan is forgiven, which could be after ten years to twenty-five years, depending on your repayment plan.

However, one important factor to consider if you are thinking about that strategy is that the amount of your student loan debt that is forgiven will be considered taxable income that year.

For instance, if after the term, your student loan payment is 40,000 dollars, that year, the 40,000 dollars will be considered taxable income. Also, keep in mind that it is hard to predict which income tax bracket you will be ten or twenty-five years in the future.

For those reasons, once you have paid off your "bad debt," it is wise to focus on aggressively working toward paying off your student loans.

My friend Melissa went to graduate school and ended up with hundreds of thousands of dollars of student loan debt.

Upon graduation, she landed a good-paying job making six figures. She also decided to aggressively pay off her student loans by living below her means. While most of her classmates expanded their lifestyles, Melissa continued to drive the car that had been in her family for over ten years. She chose to pay double the amount on her repayment schedule every month to repay her student loans faster. Melissa and her husband, Steve, also decided not to have a big wedding and instead used the money toward student loan debt repayment. Most of their family and friends do not understand their choices because, like most people, they view student loans as "good debt." However, Melissa and Steve are determined to pay off her student loans in five years. What they are doing is sacrificing the first five years of their married life to buy their freedom. Once Melissa and Steve are done paying off their student loans, they can decide how to reallocate that extra money every month. That level of discipline can only serve them in the future. Once you have developed the habit of sacrificing for five years to attain a goal, it is unlikely that you will fall victim to excessive lifestyle upgrades.

Under the first scenario, Melissa, who signed up for a ten-year income base repayment method, would pay about 1,400 dollars a month toward a student loan debt. To simplify the calculation, let's assume that her income will not change drastically during that period. After ten years, Melissa would have paid 168,000 dollars toward her student loan balance. Her estimated outstanding balance of around 70,000 dollars would be forgiven and become taxable income that year. Assuming that Melissa is in the 35 percent income tax bracket that year, she would owe 24,500 of taxes on that income.

Under the second scenario, Melissa would pay 3,000 dollars a month toward her student loan debt. After five years, she would have paid 180,000 dollars toward her balance and paid off her student loans. In the next five years, Melissa and Steve can focus on investing these 3,000 dollars a month heavily in themselves, their projects, and retirement, without having to feel bonded by debt.

Once you change your financial habits and make better money decisions, the positive results will inspire you.

Do not be embarrassed by past financial mistakes. As you work your way out of debt, you should teach your kids so they do not make the same mistakes. It is essential to share the challenges faced and the lessons learned.

I wrote this book because I realized that our community did not have the tools needed to secure its financial future. I wanted to share my knowledge and observations, and inspire Black people to make better financial decisions. There is still time to turn things around as a parent.

You can get out of debt if you change your approach and rearrange your finances. You can make sacrifices for a few years to build a better financial future for your family.

Develop a plan to free yourself from debt. Aggressively work toward paying off your student loans. Once you are free of bad debt and student loans, consider paying off your mortgage early.

Consider paying off your mortgage early.

Being free includes being debt-free, but due to the usually low interest rates associated with mortgage loans, the decision to pay off your mortgage is often not straightforward. However, whether or not to pay your mortgage early is a decision that everyone should at least consider.

The median home price of a previously owned home in the United States in 2019 was 245,000 dollars.[XI] Let us assume a 20 percent down payment, and a 4.2 percent interest rate,[XII] the average interest rate on a thirty-year (the most common) mortgage in January 2019. This would result in a monthly principal and interest payment of 958 dollars.

Let us calculate the impact of paying off your thirty-year mortgage early, and compare it to not paying it off early.

	Scenario 1	Scenario 2	Scenario 3
Payoff time	30 years	26 years	20 years
Principal and interest	$978	$978	$978
Extra payment	Never	Yearly	Quarterly
Annual extra payment ($)	0	$978	$3,912
Payoff time in years	30	26	18
Time savings	0	4	12
Total interest paid	$152,105	$126,871	$86,859
Interest savings	-	$25,223	$65,235

Scenario 1 corresponds to the thirty-year loan agreement. You make no extra payment over the thirty-year term. As a result, you will pay 152,105 dollars in interest on a 200,000 dollar loan (45,000 dollars in down payment) over thirty years.

Under scenario 2, you send one extra mortgage payment of 978 dollars. Sending that additional payment once a year over the first twenty-six years of the term would save you 25,223 dollars in interest payment. It would also allow you to pay off the mortgage in twenty-six years, which is four years early.

Under scenario 3, you send an extra mortgage payment of 978 dollars once a quarter for the first twenty years of the term of the loan. The additional payment of 978 dollars every quarter, or 3,912 dollars a year, would save you 65,235 dollars in loan interest. It would also allow you to pay off the mortgage in twenty years, which is ten years early.

The scenarios above illustrate the potential savings you could get from paying your mortgage early. However, there are pros and cons associated with that decision. The main advantages of paying off your mortgage early are having peace of mind that you own your house outright, saving a lot of money on interest, and freeing up cash that you would have otherwise used to make your mortgage payments to save or invest.

The main disadvantages of paying off your mortgage early are having a lot of money tied into your home, not taking a tax deduction for mortgage interest, and missing out on potentially higher returns from other investments.

The final decision to pay off your house early or not depends on your comfort level with having debt.

If you are interested in paying off your mortgage early, you should first ensure that you will not be subject to any prepayment penalties. However, if you think that paying your mortgage off early is not the best thing for you, you should consider at least making an extra payment once or twice a year.

CHAPTER 9

Saving for the Near Future

Building solid short and medium-term saving strategies

A key component of financial security we need to understand and teach our kids is the importance of saving. In the long run, everyone should aim to have three savings: short-term, mid-term, and long-term.

Short-term savings are funds that you keep readily available and plan to spend in the next three years. Mid-term savings are funds you anticipate needing in four to ten years. Long-term savings is money that you set aside and do not anticipate needing for at least ten years.

Saving for short-term expenses

Emergency fund

Financial setbacks happen in life in the form of unexpected car or house repairs, medical bills, layoffs, and many other ways. An emergency fund is money that you set aside in cash or cash equivalents (saving or money market account) to cover those unexpected expenses. Having cash in reserve buys you time to figure out what to do next if you end up in a difficult financial situation due to unforeseen events. You want to be prepared in the event that these types of emergencies happen. You want to avoid borrowing money or finding yourself behind on your mortgage or in any other extreme financial situation.

In early 2020, a health pandemic took the world by storm. An infectious disease caused by a new form of the coronavirus (COVID-19) spread throughout most parts of the world. Though most people exposed to the virus were expected to recover, the virus was highly contagious and spread very quickly. It resulted in death and life-threatening situations for a significant portion of the population. There were no vaccines or guaranteed cure. Hospitals around the world did not have enough equipment to face the pandemic. As a result, what was considered normal life in many parts of the world stopped. Schools closed for months while parents had to homeschool their kids, and many businesses closed temporarily and some permanently. Millions of people who were not in a position to do their work from home lost their jobs overnight.

Often, people believe that they have time to build their emergency fund. That is until a financial emergency happens, and they realize that they are not prepared for it. Part of being financially secure is having a rainy day fund, as it is impossible to predict when you will need to use it.

For years, I have talked to my family and friends about the importance of building an emergency fund. Recently, my friend Melissa had to relocate with her husband Steve, for family reasons. Melissa was able to work from another city, but her husband could not do the same. To relocate, Steve had to resign from his position and look for another job in the new city. It was a difficult decision to make, because a good portion of their income would disappear until Steve was able to find a new job. However, because Melissa and Steve had an emergency fund, they had the financial security to make the best decision for their family and relocate.

When my twins were six months old, my family had to temporarily move out of our home due to extensive water damage. The damage occurred after the fridge water line leaked. The water destroyed the hardwood floor on the main level and spread down to our basement. As a result, we had to bring in a water mitigation company to ensure that there would not be any moisture in the house. The house needed significant work to get back to its original state—which included replacing floors on two levels, and replacing ceilings and drywalls. Our family unexpectedly moved to temporary housing for seven weeks while the work was getting done at our house. Though the insurance company covered most expenses, we had to spend out of pocket as well, not only for our deductible but also for additional costs, such as having to eat out regularly during those seven weeks. During that time, my husband and I were grateful that we had an emergency fund to cover those costs. It provided relief to a very stressful situation. Water damage is one of the most common reasons people file a claim on their home insurance. However, it is something most people do not anticipate until it happens to them.

Financial experts' opinions vary on how much one needs to have in an emergency fund. But, the consensus is that you should aim to have at least three to six months of necessary living expenses in cash or cash equivalents available in your emergency fund. Suze Orman recommends having at least eight months of living expenses set aside in an emergency fund. It is a good long-term plan to consider, even if it could take years to achieve. An eight to twelve-month emergency fund would provide a substantial level of financial security to face life's unfortunate events. It would also provide you with a certain level of freedom.

If you are currently working on getting out of debt (outside of mortgage and student loans), you can start with a 1,000 dollars or so of emergency funds, while you aggressively work toward paying off your debt.

Once you have saved the first 1,000 dollars, you can aim for 2,000 dollars of savings next, and then a full month of expenses.

The next goal should be to build up your emergency fund to the equivalent of at least three months of living expenses. The process of building an emergency fund might take a significant amount of time.

It takes the average family two years to build a six-month rainy day fund. However, it is necessary to continue to work toward that goal. Once you have accumulated enough money to cover three months of your expenses, keep saving to reach at least six months of expense savings. When you face unexpected expenses, make it a goal to replenish the fund, so you are always prepared for the next unexpected expense.

Deciding if you should have more than six months of living expenses in your emergency fund depends on several factors. The nature of your employment (salaried or self-employed), the health of the company you work for, the industry you are in, and your family situation . . . are all factors you should consider. Based on your situation, you must determine how much financial cushion you need to feel secure in the event you have unexpected expenses. We must teach our Kings and Queens that though building a healthy emergency fund can take years, it is a crucial milestone to achieve on the road to financial security. We must also instill in our children that they should only use this reserve in case of an emergency. As it is not possible to predict when an emergency fund will be needed, it should not be invested. The funds should be readily available in a savings or money market account.

Below are a few steps that you can take to fund your emergency savings.
1. Open a dedicated account for emergency savings.
2. Set up weekly or monthly recurring automatic transfers between your checking account and emergency savings account. The most important thing is to start—even if it means that you can only set up recurring transfers of ten dollars right now.
3. Reduce grocery expenses by buying in bulk.
4. Cut down eating out and start meal planning.
5. Switch to a Mobile Virtual Network Operator (MVNO) cellphone plan. MVNO companies purchase wholesale voice, text, and data from the big cellphone networks. They offer plans at a lower price to customers because they do not have the overheads that the large networks have.
6. Reduce household expenses by canceling cable and unused subscriptions.
7. Shop around for better deals on home and car insurance.
8. Find items to sell on the internet.
9. Increase your income by starting a side hustle or by looking for a better job.
10. Save your tax refund.

Saving for planned expenses

Another important lesson we should teach our children is planning for large expenses that can be anticipated by setting money aside every month.

Below is a list of expenses that we can all typically expect to happen in the future.

1. Gifts

Every year, we can expect our loved ones to celebrate a birthday. There are also other occasions where families exchange gifts based on traditions. As these events happen every year, planning for them will help avoid trying to figure out how to cover the expenses and charging a credit card at the last minute.

2. Car and home repairs

When you own a car or a house, you should expect repairs in the future. You should set money aside in your budget to cover these expenses when they occur. The amount varies based on the car and home. There are a couple of rules of thumb to help you estimate the cost of home repairs. Being able to set aside 1 dollar per square foot every year, or 1 to 2 percent of your home value every year are good starting points.

For car repairs, a good starting point is to set aside the amount spent the previous year plus 10 percent.

In addition to the examples mentioned above, we should encourage our kids to plan for any significant purchase. The threshold for an expense to be considered large depends on each individual's financial situation. The most important is to encourage our youth to plan and ensure that the money is available in cash or in a cash equivalent account.

Saving for medium-term expenses

3. Down payment for a house

Homeownership is a personal decision; so is the amount of money a person decides to put as a down payment. The recommended down payment to avoid private mortgage insurance on a conventional loan is 20 percent of the purchase price —but not everyone will put that much money down. However, for reasons mentioned in the mortgage debt section of this book, buying a house with less than 10 percent of the house value as down payment can be risky as the real estate market is unpredictable.

Home prices vary considerably from one state to the next. In the United States, West Virginia is the state with the lowest median home price (108,236 dollars), while Hawaii is the state with the highest median home price (636,451 dollars). Using these prices to illustrate how much money would represent a 10 to 20 percent down payment, 10,824 to 21,647 would be needed in West Virginia instead of 63,645 to 127,290 in Hawaii. If someone plans to purchase a home in the next three years or more, it is important to set money aside every month for the down payment.

4. Saving for your dream

When I turned twenty-seven years old, I started setting money aside every month to apply toward my dream. At the time, I was unsure what the dream consisted of, or when I would pursue it. I just felt that I needed to have something to help me chase my dreams when I was ready. I wanted to have money available when I decided to follow through and fund a passion project with money not tied to an emergency fund or a retirement plan. Though it was not much, that practice gave me something to look forward to. In hindsight, I wish I had started saving toward that as soon as I started working.

We all have dreams, whether we continue to keep them in the back of our minds or are slowly letting go of them. Dreams can be anything you are interested in doing—starting a photography business, going to graduate school, or traveling to a specific destination.

What dreams do you have for yourself? Do you need to prioritize certain aspects of your life to achieve those dreams? Turning dreams to reality requires action. You need to be specific about your dreams. Setting financial goals attached to your dreams will help. Once you have written your dreams down, you can begin visualizing them. You will be more motivated to save toward your goals. The next step is to set a date when you would like to achieve that first dream.

Let us pretend that your dream is to start a side hustle in the next two years. You have estimated the initial cost to buy the material that you need and get your side business started to be 3,000 dollars. To achieve that dream within your timeline, you would need to save 125 dollars a month for the next twenty-four months. Now that you have this information, you can figure out how to include the 125 dollars in your budget. Make it a priority. Consider making automatic contributions to your dream fund; otherwise, it might become an afterthought, and might never happen.

If you are not clear on the dream yet, you should get started anyways. You can start small with 50 dollars a month and continue to ask the question to yourself. Over time, you will figure out something of interest to you. You can then assess how much you will need and adjust your budget accordingly.

One thing that has worked for me is opening a separate savings account for my dream fund. You can give the account a specific name to signal to yourself that you should not spend the money. Another way to fund your dream is to take advantage of the talent you have. Consider having an online store sell old items or your own creations on sites like Etsy.

CHAPTER 10
Saving for the Long Run

Building a successful long-term saving strategy

Preparing for traditional retirement

Assessing retirement needs

An essential part of adequately planning for retirement is estimating how much money you will need to feel financially secure when you retire. As of 2020, the retirement age in the United States of America is sixty-five years old if born before 1937 and sixty-seven years old if born in 1960 or later.

How much an individual will need to live a comfortable life at retirement depends on their lifestyle.

A common rule of thumb estimates that you should save 15 percent or more of your income every year toward your retirement. This rule of thumb assumes that you save and invest toward your retirement between the ages of twenty-five and sixty-seven.

This savings rate will set you on the right track to maintain your current lifestyle at retirement. After each income increase, you should keep your saving rate at 15 percent or more of your pre-tax income.

It is an excellent rule of thumb if you start saving for retirement on or before age twenty-five—but most people do not. Thus, they have to boost their retirement savings rates to make up the years of missed compounded interest. Sharing this valuable information with your children when they are young is critical. It will encourage them to start setting aside 15 percent or more of their income toward retirement when they start their careers. It might not be possible to save 15 percent of their entry-level income right away—but by having these ongoing discussions with them, you help keep the information in the back of their mind. They might begin with a lower percentage and increase the saving rate by 1 percent every six months or every year to reach a 15 percent saving rate or higher.

The exercise below will help you estimate and teach your young adults how much money they should have available at retirement.

I encourage you to take some time to complete this exercise. It will give you a benchmark of how much retirement savings you should aim to have. The next step would be to work diligently to set money aside for retirement—while continuing to reassess every year if your retirement savings strategy is adequate.

1. Estimate your income replacement rate

Your income replacement rate is the percentage of your income that you will need to maintain your lifestyle at retirement. According to T. Rowe Price, as a rule of thumb, you should plan an income replacement rate of 75 percent of your gross pre-retirement income.[1]

Let us assume that you are replacing an income of 80,000 dollars; the 75 percent translates into estimated annual retirement expenses of 60,000.

Let us assume that you are replacing an income of 300,000 dollars; the 75 percent translates into estimated annual retirement expenses of 225,000.

2. Use a retirement calculator

Once you have your estimated annual retirement expenses, you can use a retirement calculator.

Websites like Kiplinger or SmartAsset provide free retirement calculators. Once you input your age, expected retirement age, estimated annual retirement expenses, and how much you have already saved for retirement, the calculator will provide a recommended monthly retirement saving amount.

Using the two retirement incomes from the previous page, assuming thirty-seven years of age, here are the inputs and recommendations received from the financial calculator.

Scenario 1

- Current gross income: $80,000
- Years until retirement: 30
- Income replacement ratio: 75%
- Monthly retirement income from Social Security and other: $0
- Current retirement savings: $100,000
- Estimated average return on investments: 6% (conservative)
- Years expected to live in retirement: 25
- Percentage of portfolio invested in stocks at the beginning of retirement: conservative 35%
- Retirement Savings: $1,152/month or $13,824/year or 17.33% of gross income

Scenario 2

- Current gross income: $80,000
- Years until retirement: 30
- Income replacement ratio: 75%
- Monthly retirement income from Social Security and other: $0
- Current retirement savings: $10,000
- Estimated average return on investments: 6% (conservative)
- Years expected to live in retirement: 25
- Percentage of portfolio invested in stocks at the beginning of retirement: conservative 35%
- Retirement Savings: $1,623/month or $19,476/year or 24.4% of gross income

Under the first scenario, at thirty-seven years old, the person has saved 100,000 dollars in retirement accounts. Contributing approximately 17 percent of their income for the next thirty years should set them on track to replace 75 percent of their 80,000 dollar income at retirement. Under the second scenario, the person only has 10,000 dollars set aside in retirement accounts. They will have to save more aggressively for the next thirty years to catch up. Contributing approximately 24 percent of their income for the next thirty years should set them on track to replace 75 percent of their 80,000 dollar income at retirement.

Scenario 3

- Current gross income: $300,000
- Years until retirement: 30
- Income replacement ratio: 75%
- Monthly retirement income from Social Security and other: $0
- Current retirement savings: $400,000
- Estimated average return on investments: 6% (conservative)
- Years expected to live in retirement: 25
- Percentage of portfolio invested in stocks at the beginning of retirement: conservative 35%
- Retirement Savings: $4,191/month or $50,292/year (16.8% of gross income)

Scenario 4

- Current gross income: $300,000
- Years until retirement: 30
- Income replacement ratio: 75%
- Monthly retirement income from Social Security and other: $0
- Current retirement savings: $100,000
- Estimated average return on investments: 6% (conservative)
- Years expected to live in retirement: 25
- Percentage of portfolio invested in stocks at the beginning of retirement: conservative 35%
- Retirement Savings: $5,760/month or $69,120/year or 23.0% of gross income

Under the third scenario, at thirty-seven years old, the person has saved 400,000 dollars in retirement accounts. Contributing approximately 17 percent of their income for the next thirty years should set them on track to replace 75 percent of their 300,000 dollar income at retirement. Under the fourth scenario, the person only has 100,000 dollars set aside in retirement accounts. They will have to save more aggressively for the next thirty years to catch up. Contributing approximately 23 percent of their income for the next thirty years should set them on track to replace 75 percent of their 300,000 dollar income at retirement.

Tracking your retirement progress

Once in a year, you should review your retirement savings and assess your progress.

Fidelity's** rule of thumb is to have one time your starting salary saved for retirement by age thirty, three times your income by age forty, six times by age fifty, eight times by age sixty, and ten times by age sixty-seven.

Saving and investing for your retirement is necessary to reach financial security. Assessing your progress every year is also very important to ensure that you are on the right track. The exercises above are rules of thumb—starting points for your planning. Saving and investing even more would get you in better shape when retirement comes. By deciding to work diligently at saving and investing toward retirement, you will send a signal to your kids that they should not worry about their parents' financial needs—they should instead aggressively focus on building their financial future.

Retirement accounts

A crucial part of raising financially secure kids is educating our kids, particularly our young adults, about the importance of setting money aside for the long term, especially for life after work. According to a report produced by the Federal Reserve Bank, in 2018, one-quarter of all American adults had no retirement savings.[ii] Saving for retirement is often put on the backburner by young professionals. However, the time value of money is a significant factor in favor of starting to save for retirement early.

We should teach our children the importance of starting to save for retirement early. We should also introduce them to the most common ways they can set money aside for their retirement.

The types of accounts below are the most common retirement accounts in the United States. If you live in a different country, you can review the description of the accounts and investigate whether or not equivalent or similar retirement accounts are available in the country where you reside.

Company-sponsored 401(k) plan

A 401(k) is an investment retirement plan offered by an employer as a retirement benefit. In 2020, the maximum amount an employee under fifty years old can contribute to a 401K plan per year is 19,500 dollars (26,000 dollars if fifty or older).

** Fidelity is a financial services company that manages more than thirty million retirement accounts.

Employees can elect to contribute part of their paycheck to their 401(k) with before- (traditional 401(k)) or after-tax dollars (Roth 401(k)).

With a traditional 401(k), the employee elects to defer taxes on contributions and earnings until retirement (age fifty-nine-and-a-half or later). This allows the money to grow without incurring taxes until retirement. As distributions are taken at retirement, Federal and State income taxes will be owed. With a Roth 401(k), the employee chooses to pay taxes on contributions upfront so the investment can grow tax-free. Withdrawals are made without incurring any additional taxes as long as they are made at age fifty-nine-and-a-half or later.

The pros and cons of the traditional and Roth options are discussed later in this chapter.

Most young adults who begin their careers in their twenties at entry-level salaries are not concerned about retirement. They believe that they have the luxury of time and can start saving for retirement when their income increases. However, delaying the decision to start saving for retirement means losing the monetary benefits of the time value of money; and it often also means leaving free money from an employer on the table. Indeed, many employers offer matching retirement contributions to a company-provided 401(k) plan up to a certain percentage of the employee's salary. As of 2019, the average 401(k) company match was 4.7 percent of an employee's salary.[III]

According to the National Association of Colleges and Employers (NACE) in their Summer 2019 Salary Survey report, the average starting salary for 2018 was 50,944 dollars.[IV]

To get the average 4.7 percent company match, an employee would need to contribute 2,394 dollars of the 50,944 dollars salary. That is approximately 100 dollars every two weeks, or 50 dollars a week.

This investment of 2,394 dollars would translate to 4,788 dollars (after the company match) in retirement savings in the first year. That 4,788 dollars first-year investment can turn into about 78,000 dollars at retirement, assuming a 7 percent return (S&P 500 historical annual return of 8 percent adjusted for inflation) without adding a cent. The objective is that after a year of investing in their employee retirement accounts to get the company match, they will develop the habit and continue to invest in the future.

We can use this as an illustration of the importance of retirement planning for our kids. We should communicate the importance of taking advantage of a company's retirement contribution match to our kids. If our young adults do not feel that they are in a financial situation to start saving money for retirement, we should emphasize the value they would get from at least contributing to get the maximum amount of money from the company match.

Solo 401(k) plan

A solo or one participant 401(k) is a retirement investment plan for a self-employed person or business owner without any full-time employee(s).

With this plan, business owners can contribute to a solo 401(k) as both the employer and employee.

In 2020, as an employee under fifty years old, you can contribute up to 19,500 dollars per year (26,000 dollars if fifty or older), to your solo 401(k) plan. Additionally, as the employer, you can make a profit-sharing contribution—up to 25 percent of the compensation you receive from the business. Your total employer and employee contribution should not exceed 57,000 dollars per year (63,500 per year if fifty or older).

A spouse, who receives their income from the business, can also contribute to the account and receive an employer contribution. The same contribution limits mentioned above are followed (57,000 dollars per year of total employee and employer contribution if under fifty years old, and 63,500 per year if fifty or older).

In a solo 401(k) plan, all contributions you make as the employer are tax-deductible to your business with all earnings growing tax-deferred until withdrawn. For the contributions you make as the employee, you can decide whether to contribute pre-tax or after-tax dollars. The same early withdrawal penalties under a company-sponsored 401(k) apply under a solo 401(k) plan.

A solo 401(k) is an option if your kids are young entrepreneurs or are interested in entrepreneurship.

With a solo 401(k) plan, they can maximize business deductions and contribute toward retirement.

403(b)

A 403(b), also called a tax-sheltered annuity (TSA), is a similar investment retirement plan to a 401(k). They are offered to employees working for public schools and specific tax-exempt organizations. As of 2020, employees under fifty years old can contribute up to 19,500 dollars per year (26,000 dollars if fifty or older) to a 403(b) account. Employee contributions are deducted directly from the employee's paycheck (pre-tax dollars). Employers can also contribute to a former employee's account five years after the date of severance—up to the annual limit (with total contributions not exceeding 57,000 dollars in 2020).

Contributions and earnings grow tax-deferred until retirement (age fifty-nine-and-a-half or later). At retirement, you will owe state and federal income taxes on the withdrawal amount.

457(b)

A 457(b), also known as a deferred compensation plan, is an employer-sponsored investment plan offered to state and local government employees as well as a few tax-exempt organizations.

Employees and employers can contribute to the 457(b) plan. In 2020, the annual contribution limit for employees under fifty is 19,500 dollars (26,000 dollars if fifty or older) to a 457(b) account.

Also, within three years of the "normal retirement age" specified in the plan, employees can contribute the lesser of twice the normal elective deferral limit (39,000 dollars in 2020), or the basic annual limit plus the amount of the basic annual limit not used in prior years. It is applicable as long as they are contributing no less than 19,500 dollars a year.

Like a 401(k), money contributed to a 457(b) account to financial investments can be in pre-tax or after-tax dollars.

Contributions and earnings grow tax-deferred until retirement (age sixty or later) if you choose to contribute in pre-tax dollars. Earnings grow tax-free if you decide to contribute in after-tax dollars.

Individual Retirement Accounts (IRA)

An Individual Retirement Account is a tax-favored investment account for retirement. Only earned income in the current year can be contributed to an individual retirement account. An individual can open an IRA account at most brokerage firms such as Vanguard, Fidelity, or TD Ameritrade.

As the IRA is not a company-sponsored plan, the individual has more flexibility in terms of the investment options. In an IRA account, you can opt to invest in individual stocks, bonds, mutual funds, exchange-traded funds (ETF), and other types of investments from the provider of your choice.

You do not encounter the common limitations set by employers in a company-sponsored retirement account, such as purchasing from a single provider or selecting investments from a list of company-approved investments.

There are two main types of IRA accounts: the traditional IRA and the Roth IRA.

The individual annual contribution limit in all IRA accounts combined is 6,000 dollars in 2020 if an individual is under fifty years old (or 7,000 dollars if over the age of fifty).

Traditional IRA

A traditional individual retirement account lets you postpone your taxes until retirement (at age fifty-nine-and-a-half or later).

Any contributions and earnings in a traditional deductible IRA account will grow tax-deferred until retirement, at which point they will be taxed at your ordinary income tax rate.

If your employer or your spouse's employer offers an employer-sponsored retirement plan, your pre-tax contribution to a traditional IRA plan might be limited. Your Modified Adjusted Gross Income (MAGI) determines whether your contributions will be deductible on your tax returns.

Your modified adjusted gross income (MAGI) determines your eligibility to contribute to a Roth IRA account. Your modified adjusted gross income is your adjusted gross income (gross income minus eligible deductions) plus a few adjustments, such as tax-exempt interest or deductible higher education expenses that are added back. Your MAGI is usually very close to your AGI, as most of the deductions that are added back are not common deductions.

You should still explore that option if you are only eligible to make contributions to a nondeductible IRA as opposed to a deductible IRA. It will allow you to set aside additional dollars for retirement with tax-deferred earnings until retirement.

Contributions in a traditional deductible IRA account are in post-tax dollars. As such, only earnings will be taxed as ordinary income as you make withdrawals at retirement. For that reason, keeping good track of your contributions is essential. When you begin taking distributions at retirement, it will help ensure that your contributions are not subject to ordinary income taxes.

Roth IRA

A Roth IRA is an individual retirement account in which contributions are in after-tax dollars. Earnings grow tax-free, and all withdrawals made at retirement are tax-free.

In 2020, the (MAGI) limit to be able to contribute the maximum amount to a Roth IRA account (6,000 dollars a year or 7,000 dollars if over fifty years old) is 124,000 dollars for an individual, and 196,000 dollars for a married couple filing jointly. A formula must be used to determine the amount of the partial Roth IRA contribution allowed with MAGI—between 124,000 and 139,000 dollars for an individual and 196,000 and 206,000 dollars for a married couple filing jointly.

If your income is above the limit to contribute to a Roth IRA, you can use the backdoor Roth IRA strategy. High-income earners can contribute after-tax money to a traditional nondeductible IRA and then convert the contributions to a Roth IRA every year. You should consider using a backdoor ROTH strategy if you do not qualify for a Roth IRA. All Roth IRA withdrawals are tax-free at retirement; it would, at minimum, simplify the tax process.

Another advantage of a Roth IRA is qualified distributions. Qualified distributions allow an individual to withdraw from a Roth IRA account tax and penalty-free at any time as long as it does not exceed the sum of everything they have put in up until that point. Knowing that you can withdraw contributions from an IRA without incurring additional taxes or any penalties is a good safety net. However, as the goal is to save for retirement, you should refrain from withdrawing money from your Roth IRA unless it is the only option.

Self-directed IRA

A self-directed IRA allows you to save for retirement with pre-tax or post-tax dollars. The annual contribution limits and eligibility requirements for a self-directed IRA are the same as a traditional or Roth IRA. However, with a self-directed IRA, in addition to the typical investments under a standard IRA account, an individual can also invest in alternative assets (real estate, non-traded businesses, cryptocurrencies, and precious metals, for instance). The account holder directly manages a self-directed IRA, though a qualified IRA custodian or trustee must hold the account.

Due to the research and due diligence needed to manage a self-directed IRA effectively, this type of account is typically used by more savvy investors.

Savings Incentive Match Plan for Employees IRA (SIMPLE IRA)

A Savings Incentive Match Plan for Employees or Simple IRA is a retirement plan for small businesses. You might be eligible for a savings incentive matched plan if the company you work for has one hundred employees or less, and you have earned a minimum of 5,000 dollars from the company in the past two years.

As of 2020, the maximum amount an employee under fifty years old can contribute per year is 13,500 dollars (16,500 dollars if age fifty or older). Employers are also required to match employees' contributions up to 3 percent of employee's compensation or contribute 2 percent of employee compensation to participate in the plan. In the simple IRA, your contributions are in pre-tax dollars.

If you are self-employed, you can contribute as both the employee and employer. Earnings grow tax-deferred until withdrawals. All withdrawals will be subject to ordinary federal and state income taxes at retirement (age fifty-nine-and-a-half or later).

Any early withdrawal would be subject to a 10 or 25 percent penalty if made within two years of opening the plan, in addition to the ordinary income taxes.

Simplified Employee Pension IRA (SEP-IRA)

A Simplified Employee Pension plan is a retirement plan for small businesses with several employees or self-employed individuals. Contributions to a SEP-IRA or Salary Reduction Simplified Employee Pension Plan (SARSEP), a SEP plan set up before 1997 are made by the employer directly for each employee on a pre-tax basis.

In 2020, employers can contribute up to a quarter of an employee's compensation, not to exceed 57,000 dollars.

As a business owner, the percentage of your compensation that you contribute to your account must match the percentage that you contribute to other employees' accounts. SEP Earnings grow tax-deferred until withdrawals. All withdrawals will be subject to ordinary federal and state income taxes at retirement (age fifty-nine-and-a-half or later).

Health Savings Account (HSA)

A Health Savings Account or HSA is a tax advantage account designed to help save for medical expenses not covered by high-deductible health plans. An individual must be enrolled in a high-deductible health insurance plan to qualify for an HSA.

Contributions to an HSA plan are tax-deductible and remain in your account until used. Both employer and employee can contribute to an HSA. Contributions can be invested in stocks and mutual funds, among other options. The investment and withdrawals grows tax-free until retirement. However, if the money is used for non-eligible expenses, you will incur ordinary income taxes and a 10 percent penalty if you are under the age of sixty-five. As of 2020, the maximum annual contribution to an HSA account is 3,550 dollars for individuals and 7,100 for families. An additional 1,000 dollars contribution is allowed per year for individuals fifty-five or older.

Pre-tax versus after-tax contributions

As mentioned earlier in the chapter, some retirement accounts give you the option to contribute pre-tax dollars (traditional) or after-tax dollars (Roth) to the account. There are pros and cons to both options.

When you choose to contribute with before-tax dollars, your investment will grow tax-deferred until the money is withdrawn at retirement (in most cases at fifty-nine-and-a-half or later). For the retirement accounts mentioned previously (except HSA accounts), at retirement, you will owe state and federal income taxes on the withdrawal amounts (contributions and earnings).

If you were to withdraw money before that age, you would also incur a 10 percent penalty in most cases, and pay income taxes.

With pre-tax dollar contributions, your yearly contributions lower your taxable income. When contributing pre-tax dollars to a retirement plan, most people assume that they will be in a similar or lower income tax bracket at retirement. However, it can be hard to predict which income tax bracket you will be in at retirement, depending on how far retirement is for you.

Younger people are often encouraged to pay taxes upfront by contributing after-tax dollars to their retirement plans, because their income tax brackets might increase drastically by the time they retire. Following the same reasoning, people close to retirement are often encouraged to take advantage of the before-tax contribution option, because they are more likely to have a good idea of their retirement income tax bracket. Deciding to contribute before or after-tax dollars is a personal decision. One must be informed about the pros and cons of each option before making an educated decision.

Early withdrawal penalties

Most retirement accounts have penalties if withdrawals are made before the retirement age of fifty-nine-and-a-half. For 401(k), 403(b), and IRA accounts, a 10 percent penalty is standard—but it can go up to 25 percent if the withdrawal is made within two years of opening a SIMPLE IRA account.

An individual can withdraw money from their 401(k) account penalty-free for financial emergency events before age fifty-nine-and-a-half. The following are examples that qualify as an emergency:

- Purchase of a primary residence
- Eviction or foreclosure prevention
- Loss-related repairs on a primary residence
- Out-of-pocket medical expenses
- Postsecondary education
- Funeral or burial expenses.

To withdraw the money penalty-free, the participant must demonstrate that all other financing options have been exhausted, and the distribution is necessary to face the financial emergency.

For 403(b) plans, distributions before age fifty-nine-and-a-half are subject to a 10 percent early withdrawal penalty and taxes, but an employee can take loans and hardship distributions. However, a penalty-free withdrawal can happen if any of the following circumstances occur:

1. Employment severance
2. Disability
3. Death
4. Financial hardship.

Withdrawals before age fifty-nine-and-a-half from individual retirement accounts will usually trigger a 10 percent penalty unless they qualify under withdrawal exceptions. A few examples of the withdrawal exceptions which would waive the penalty include:

- Medical expenses exceeding 10 percent of adjusted gross income and not covered by health insurance
- Healthcare insurance in case you are unemployed

- College-related expenses
- First home purchase
- Disability-related expenses
- Roth IRA withdrawal up to the total contributions made.

For 457(b) plans, distributions before age seventy-and-a-half are subject to a 10 percent early withdrawal penalty.

Money saved in a 457(b) can be withdrawn without penalty before age seventy-and-a-half under the following unforeseen emergency distributions:

- Plan termination
- Employment severance
- Unforeseeable emergency
- Small account distribution
- Permissible eligible automatic contribution arrangement withdrawals within the time stated in the plan
- Qualified domestic relations order (retirement plan split as a result of a judicial order in a divorce or legal property division).

For all of the retirement plans mentioned above, if a plan participant could get the early withdrawal penalty waived, the plan participant would still incur income taxes (if applicable) for the amount withdrawn.

This chapter highlights different ways to save for retirement. You can decide which of these options best suits your situation. It is essential to set specific goals and assess your progress every year to determine if you are on track toward your retirement savings and adjust your strategy accordingly.

Exploring FIRE

Financial Independence (F.I.) is when you have enough passive income or investments to cover your living expenses for the rest of your life. When you reach financial independence, you have the option to stop trading your time for money. You can choose to focus your energy on the things that matter to you with money taking a backseat, because you do not need to generate income to sustain your lifestyle. Financial independence gives you more freedom to do what matters to you in life.

The Financial Independence Retire Early (FIRE) movement originated in the early 1990s with the book *Your Money or Your Life* by Vicki Robin, Joe Dominguez, and Monique Tilford. The authors introduced the idea that people should reach for financial independence earlier in life to enjoy the best years of their lives, instead of being forced to continue to trade their time for money.

The FIRE movement, which started gaining momentum around the world in the mid-2000s, emphasizes saving aggressively and investing. The FIRE philosophy encourages you to optimize your lifestyle and spend money on what matters to you.

In the FIRE community, the "Four Percent Rule" and "Multiply by 25" rules are often used as baselines to determine your FIRE number. The Four Percent Rule assumes a return on your portfolio of 7 percent, and factors approximately 3 percent for inflation. It was created based on stock and bond returns over fifty years. The idea is that you can withdraw 4 (7 rate of return-3 inflation = 4) percent of your portfolio every year without touching your principal amount.

The multiply by 25 rule estimates your retirement needs by multiplying your annual expenses by twenty-five. It represents the amount to apply the Four Percent Rule to. When you have accumulated twenty-five times your yearly expenses, you are considered to be financially independent.

As such, the first step to determining your F.I. number is to know your annual expenses. You then multiply those expenses by twenty-five to get your financial independence number.

Based on the F.I. formula, you reach financial independence, once you have saved up twenty-five times your annual spending.

Financial Independence = annual expenses * 25

As an example, if your living expenses are 30,000 dollars a year, you will reach your F.I. number once your investments have reached 750,000 dollars. However, it does not mean that you need to save 750,000 dollars.

Let us assume that you are twenty-five years old, starting with an initial investment of 5,000 dollars, and your goal is to reach F.I. by forty-five years old.

Assuming a 6 percent return on your portfolio over the next twenty years, using a retirement calculator reveals that you would need to save a little less than 20,000 dollars a year to reach F.I. at forty-five.

Twenty thousand dollars a year can be a significant amount of money to save depending on income. However, once you know why you are interested in pursuing F.I., and you have an idea of the sacrifices necessary to reach it, you can begin to think about how to achieve that goal.

Once you have calculated your annual expenses, you can use a free finance calculator on the internet to determine how much you would need to save every year, based on your initial investment, target FIRE number, and estimated years until retirement.

There are a few things to consider when calculating your financial independence number. The Four Percent Rule assumes that your investments will generate a 7 percent long-term annualized return rate, which will translate into a 4 percent real rate after 3 percent of inflation. 7 percent is a reasonable assumption consistent with the average annual return of the stock market between 1950 and 2009. However, given that people close to retirement and retirees typically keep their portfolio in lower-return investments, a 7 percent annualized return is a bit aggressive for people who are within a few years from reaching financial independence or retirement. Also, rising healthcare expenses and unexpected events are not accounted for under these rules. Healthcare expenses usually increase later in life, and unexpected events can happen at any point in time. However, if you have assets outside of the market that generate passive income, that should reduce the amount of money you need to reach FIRE.

Most followers of the FIRE movement are aware of the risks. While some people opt to adopt a minimalist lifestyle upon retirement, "lean fire," others aim for a higher level of future spending, "fat fire." Some people use the "Multiply by 33 Rule" and a "Three Percent Rule" for precautionary measures. Under these rules, the assumptions are a 6 percent annualized long-term return rate and a real return of 3 percent after 3 percent of inflation. Some members of the FIRE movement choose to have other passive income sources to compensate for the risks. Others redirect their lives after reaching FIRE and find creative ways to continue to earn income while maintaining their freedom.

"Mr. Money Mustache" is a former software engineer who retired after working for nine years. "Mr. Money Mustache" and his wife started their careers in their early twenties, earning approximately 40,000 dollars a year. Throughout their career, "Mr. and Mrs. Money Mustache" averaged about 134,000 dollars in combined annual income. They retired nine years later, with combined annual earnings of around 170,000 dollars. However, the couple chose a frugal lifestyle, spending approximately 30,000 to 40,000 dollars a year. They consistently invested their savings on a dollar-cost average base in stock market index funds. They opted for a traditional retirement in their early thirties, with a mortgage-free house valued at around 200,000 dollars and a stock market portfolio with a value of approximately 600,000 dollars (24,000 annual expenses * 25 = 600,000 dollars).

At retirement, the couple also had real estate income of about 28,000 dollars a year to supplement the 24,000 dollars they could withdraw from their portfolio every year. Mr. Money Mustache is recognized as one of the leaders of the FIRE movement. Since traditional retirement fifteen years ago, he has focused his energy on his areas of interest, such as philanthropy and writing. He is running a very successful blog, and his creativity has allowed him to generate income and grow the couple's nest egg postretirement.

Amon and Christina Browing were federal employees with two kids who retired at the ages of forty-one and thirty-nine, respectively. The couple discovered the FIRE movement eight years before their retirement. After discovering the FIRE movement, the couple reduced their spending, notably by moving into a smaller house, and mastering travel hacking. They also focused on earning more money through real estate investments, side hustles such as driving Uber and Lift, and buying and selling items online. During that time, the couple invested 70 percent of their income and accumulated 2,000,000 dollars in assets. They went on to early retirement in 2019. They have been sharing their F.I. journey on their YouTube channel. They also recently moved to Portugal to take advantage of a better quality of life for their family.

The "Physician on Fire" retired from his career as an anesthesiologist at forty-three years old. After reaching FIRE, he continued to work on a part-time basis for a few years, until he was ready to retire. The Physician on Fire estimated his family of four's target retirement to be thirty-six times their annual spending at 2,500,000 dollars.

He walked away from a yearly income of around 400,000 dollars to avoid being a burned-out doctor, and to spend more time with his family.

The Physician on Fire developed an interest in financial education. He now enjoys educating his fellow physicians on personal finance and financial independence via his website—and donates 50 percent of the site's proceeds to charitable causes. The remaining 50 percent generates enough income to cover his family's annual expenses. As a result, his portfolio has continued to grow since "retirement."

Financial independence gives you more time and freedom to do what matters to you in life. It is about having the option to only focus on getting paid for work that you would do for free.

They are ways to achieve financial independence outside of investing in the stock market. As noted earlier in this chapter, any passive income that you will receive, such as retirement benefits or real estate income, should be taken into account on your journey to financial independence.

However, the Four Percent and Multiply by 25 Rules are a great starting point for assessing what you would need to reach financial independence. I encourage you to calculate your F.I. number. You can then adjust the number based on factors that apply to you. For instance, you can increase your F.I. number by multiplying by 36 like the physician on fire to plan for higher dependent costs and healthcare expenses to account for out-of-pocket insurance costs or to include for a more conservative annual rate of return. You can also decrease the number based on whether you plan to have other sources of passive income or plan to continue to work.

Calculating your F.I. number is a significant first step that will inspire you to set goals that can help you reach that objective.

Saving for post-education expenses

Most parents would love for their kids to attend college, but education can be costly. Helping your kids pay for college, whether in part or in full, is a nice gesture to give them a head start in life. Unfortunately, not every parent can afford to do it. If you are in a position where you can think about saving for your kids' education, starting to save early would be wise by saving and investing to take advantage of compounded interest.

The majority of parents have to prioritize financial goals between paying off debt, saving for their children's education, and investing for retirement. Having a healthy emergency fund and paying off any toxic debt may have to take priority over saving for your kids' college education. Ideally, you can balance saving for your retirement and saving for your children's college education. If you can only do one at this time, you should focus on saving for your retirement—until you can increase your income and contribute more toward your kids' college education. While there are other ways for your kids to pay for college, such as scholarships, grants, or even student loans, you will not have similar opportunities to fund your retirement. Do not compromise saving and investing in your retirement. Financially preparing for your future after the workplace is one of the best gifts you can give to your adult children. You will avoid becoming a financial burden to them while also teaching them how important it is to prepare for retirement. This chapter covers different ways to help save for your child's college education or any other postsecondary education they might be interested in pursuing—and ways to reduce the cost of going to college.

Saving for postsecondary education

529 plans

In the United States, 529 plans are among the most common ways to save for your children's education. Contributions to a 529 plan are in after-tax dollars, but the earnings grow tax-free. When you withdraw the money, it will be tax-free as long as you spend it on qualified education expenses. As of 2020, qualified expenses include, but are not limited to, tuition and fees for college and postsecondary training institutions, books and supplies, computers and internet access fees, room and board for college. Qualified expenses also include tuition expenses for K-12 schools up to 10,000 dollars a year.

There are federal income taxes, and a 10 percent penalty on plan earnings for using 529 funds for nonqualified education expenses. However, when a beneficiary receives a full scholarship to attend college, the 10 percent penalty is waived, and only the taxes are applicable. There are additional exceptions that can result in the waiver of the 10 percent penalty, but noneducational expenses will result in federal taxes on the earnings. It is crucial to keep a good record of your 529 expenses, considering that you have to report them to the IRS.

There are no income limits for 529 plan contributions, but there are limits on total account balance that varies by state, with the lowest being Georgia and Mississippi at 235,000 dollars as of 2020.

Pros:

- Money grows tax-free
- Withdrawals are tax-free as long as they are for qualified expenses
- No income limits
- High contribution maximums up to 500,000 dollars in some states
- Family members and friends can contribute up to 15,000 dollars per year without incurring IRS gift taxes
- Flexibility to change the beneficiary to another family member.

Cons:

- Taxes and 10 percent penalty for noneducational withdrawals
- Limited investment options
- Eligibility to participate in need-based financial aid may be affected.

529 plans allow you to change the beneficiary to another family member. So if the beneficiary does not attend secondary education, you can use the funds for a sibling or another family member without penalty. When looking for a 529 plan, it is best to pick a plan that gives you the option to choose your investment funds.

After realizing that parents wanted more specific guidelines on how much to save for college, Fidelity introduced the "2K rule of thumb." Assuming that parents are saving for college using a 529 plan, Fidelity recommends multiplying your child's age by two thousand to ensure that you are on track to cover half of the average four-year Public University cost. When the child goes to college at eighteen, the 2K rule of thumb assumes that the remaining 50 percent of college expenses will be covered by financial aid, family earnings, and student loans.

For instance, based on this rule of thumb, if your child is six years old, you should have 12,000 dollars or 2,000 * 6 years to feel confident that you are on the right track when it comes to college savings. However, the rule of thumb only estimates that you have enough to cover 50 percent of the cost. While some people's objective is to help their kids pay for college, others aim to cover 100 percent of college costs so they can start life debt-free. This formula serves as a good starting point. You can make adjustments based on your personal goals regarding college savings. This formula is a good tool to use every year to assess if you are on the right track as far as college savings is concerned.

Coverdell Education Savings Account

A Coverdell Education Saving is a type of account to encourage saving for education-related expenses. Coverdell Education Savings accounts are very similar to 529 plans—providing tax-free investment growth and tax-free withdrawals on qualified education expenses. But, they offer a more extensive range of investment options than a 529. Coverdell Education Savings accounts have little to no effect on financial aid eligibility, no matter who owns the account. By opening a Coverdell Education Savings account with a self-directed IRA provider, your investments can include financial securities, precious metals, real estate, private notes, and other nontraditional investments. This option is more attractive for parents with good investment knowledge.

There are a few notable disadvantages to having a Coverdell Education Saving Account. There is a maximum annual contribution limit on this account of 2,000 dollars a year as of 2020. There is also an annual modified adjusted gross income (MAGI) limit for eligibility to contribute. The ability to contribute phases out at 110,000 dollars a year for individuals, and 190,000 dollars a year for married couples filing jointly. Also, contributions to a Coverdell Education Savings account must be made before the beneficiary turns eighteen and has to be used before their thirtieth birthday.

Pros:

- Money grows tax-free
- Withdrawals are tax-free as long as they are for qualified expenses
- Extensive investment options
- Little to no effect on financial aid eligibility.

Cons:

- Annual contribution is limited
- MAGI determines eligibility
- Contributions have to be made before beneficiary's eighteenth birthday
- Withdrawals must be before beneficiary's thirtieth birthday.
- Taxes and 10 percent penalty for noneducational withdrawals.

Roth IRA

The main objective of a Roth IRA account is to prepare for retirement. As such, you can find additional details on the functioning of Roth IRA accounts in the book's "Traditional Retirement" section. However, a Roth IRA account is also an option used to save for higher education-related expenses.

Roth IRA accounts offer tax-free growth and tax-free retirement withdrawals. When using an IRA to fund higher education for yourself, a spouse, child, or grandchild, the early withdrawal penalty is waived. Roth IRA contributions grow tax-free until retirement age—but earnings are usually taxed and penalized if withdrawn before age fifty-nine-and-a-half. A Roth IRA gives you more flexibility than a 529 plan—which can only be used for qualified education expenses to avoid penalties. With the Roth IRA, you can decide later to use some of the money you saved toward your child's education—as long as you are on track for retirement. It also provides more investment options than a 529. Another advantage of the Roth IRA is that retirement accounts do not count as assets for financial aid applications. However, the year after a Roth distribution, the distribution is considered part of the student's income that year. Roth IRA accounts have maximum annual contribution limits of 6,000 dollars a year (or 7,000 dollars if over fifty years old), and yearly income limits of 124,000 dollars for individual contributors, and 196,000 dollars for married couples filing jointly, before it begins phasing out.

Pros:

- Money grows tax-free until retirement
- Not limited to educational expenses
- Withdrawal of contributions at any time penalty and tax-free
- Account balances do not have an impact on financial aid eligibility
- Taxes and 10 percent penalty for non-educational withdrawals.

Cons:

- Annual contribution is limited
- MAGI determines eligibility
- Distributions are considered part of student income
- Taxes and 10 percent penalty for early earnings withdrawal.

UGMA or UTMA accounts

Uniform Gift to Minors Accounts and Uniform Transfer to Minors Accounts are custodial accounts permitting the transfer of assets to minor recipients. UGMA and UTMA accounts are used while the child is a minor. An account custodian is selected to manage the assets or investments on behalf of the minor child. Contributions to these accounts are in after-tax dollars. The account custodian is any adult or professional asset manager that you select, including yourself. He or she can withdraw funds to cover expenses related to the well-being and education of the minor. Once the child reaches adulthood, the assets are irrevocably transferred to him free of any conditions. Parents often used UGMA and UTMA accounts for college savings—mainly because they are easy to manage and can result in tax savings when taxed at the child's tax rate. There are no contributions or income limits on UGMA and UTMA accounts.

The main difference between UGMA and UTMA accounts is the type of investment you can have. UGMA accounts are limited to cash, mutual funds, stocks, bonds, and other financial instruments, while UTMA accounts can hold any property, including real estate. You should review your state laws when it comes to UTMA accounts. UGMA accounts are available in every state, while some states do not offer UTMA accounts.

Pros:

- Potential tax savings when taxed at child's rate
- No contribution or income limits
- Easy to manage
- Not limited to child's educational expenses
- UTMA allows a wide variety of investments

Cons:

- Funds irrevocably transferred to the child at majority regardless of financial acumen
- Beneficiary must be minor
- UGMA limited investments variety
- UTMA not available in every state.

Real estate

Real estate is not a popular way to save for kids' college education—but similar to stock investing, real estate has a good record of long-term steady returns. Real estate is a good long-term investment that might coincide with your college savings timeline—if you can finance a property over a fifteen-year term.

There are three common strategies to consider when looking into real estate as a college investment.

Option 1: Sell the property after fifteen years.
Property purchase price: $160,000
Down payment: $32,000

Interest rate: 5% (typically 1 percent higher than interest rate on main residence)
Term: 15 years
Principal & Interest: $1,012
Taxes + Insurance: $187
Regular maintenance and repairs: $167
Capital expenditures:** $145
Total monthly payment: $1,511

According to U.S. Census data collected from 1963 to 2008, home prices increased by approximately 5 percent annually.

Let us be conservative and assume a 2 percent appreciation every year. Based on that assumption, the expected value in fifteen years, when you have paid off the property, would be 215,339 dollars. To calculate how much you would walk away with from the sale, you need to deduct the sales transaction price and your initial down payment from the sale. If you have taken tax benefits for depreciation of the property over the past fifteen years, you need to add it back to the profit. As noted in the real estate chapter, the IRS considers that a real estate asset has a useful life of twenty-seven-and-a-half years. As such, annual depreciation on this property is 160,000 dollars / 27.5 = $5,818.18

Sales price = $210,000
Purchase price = $160,000
15-year depreciation = $87,273
Property tax basis after commissions (6% of sales price) and depreciation recapture = $160,000 − $12,600 - $87,273 = $60,127
Gain basis = $210,000 - $60,127 = $149,873
Recapture tax rate 25% = $87,273 * 25% = $21,818.25
Capital gain taxes assuming the highest tax rate of 20% = ($149,873 − $87,273) *20% = $62,600 *0.2 = $12,520
Total taxes = $34,338.25
$210,000 − ($12,600 + $34,338.25) = $163,061.75

After selling the property, paying transaction fees, and taxes, you would have approximately $163,062 to pay for college after fifteen years.

** Refer to the "Building Wealth through Real Estate" (cash flow) section of the chapter to see the capital expenditures calculation.

Option 2: Refinance the property after fifteen years
When your child is ready to go to college, you can take money out of the property and refinance. The main advantage of refinancing as opposed to selling the property is that you avoid paying capital gain taxes. However, you would incur refinancing fees, as well as interest payments on the loan. You would also add debt to a property that was already debt-free.

Property purchase price: $160,000
Down payment: $32,000
Interest rate: 5% (typically 1 percent higher than interest rate on main residence)
Term: 15 years
Principal & Interest: $1,012
Taxes + Insurance: $187
Regular maintenance and repairs: $167
Capital expenditures: $145
Property management fee (10%) if you decide to turn over management of the property: $170
Total monthly payment: $1,681

Rent: $1,750

Cash flow = $1,700 - $1,681 = $69 / month
Cash flow = $828/year
$828*15 years = $12,420 potential savings over 15-year-period

It is always a good idea to run your numbers, assuming a property management fee. If you decide to turn over management of your property at the time of purchase or in the future, you will not have to worry about potentially having negative cash flow.

Let us be conservative and only assume 2 percent appreciation every year. Based on that assumption, the expected value in fifteen years, when you have paid off the property, would be $215,339.

Refinance inspection property value: $200,000
Let us assume you take $120,000 out for college and leave $80,000 in, 40 percent, as a down payment.

With an 80,000 dollars down payment, monthly mortgage and other fees should be approximately the same. It is safe to assume that the investment will remain cash flow positive in the future unless a significant event occurs. Indeed, over time, expenses such as property taxes and repairs will increase—but rent will also increase as the cost of living increases.

Option 3: Pay off the property and hold during college
Purchase price: $160,000
Down payment: $32,000
Interest rate: 5% (typically 1 percent higher than interest rate on main residence)
Term: 15 years
Principal & Interest: $1,012
Taxes + Insurance: $187
Regular Maintenance and repairs: $167
Capital expenditures: $145
Property management fee (10%) if you decide to turn over management of the property: $170
Total monthly payment: $1,681

Rent: $1,750

Let us assume you bought the property before your child's third birthday. The property will be paid off by the time the child goes to college fifteen years later. As you will no longer have a mortgage on the property, the cash flow will increase (1,012 dollars for principal and interest).

Cash flow = $1,750 - $1,681 + $1,012 = $1,081/month
Cash flow = $12,972/year

Above is the potential cash flow that the property could produce every year once paid off. Approximately 13,000 dollars could be available every year. In this example, though it is highly unlikely, rent is kept at the same amount for fifteen years without a single increase. This conservative approach helps compensate for expected expenses increase due to inflation and the age of the property.

Real estate is a strategy to consider to help pay for your kids' college education. The specific long-term real estate strategy that you decide to use depends on your long-term objectives. If you are strictly looking to save to pay for college, then you might not want to hold on to the property after your kids graduate from college.

If you are also looking to use the property as a source of passive income for retirement or to help your young adult learn about real estate, it might make more sense to keep the property. While in college, your child could help manage the property. When they graduate from college, you might consider refinancing or selling the property. If you are in a position to afford it, you can use some of the proceeds to help your adult child with a down payment for their own property or even gift them with the property as a graduation present.

Real estate can be a good investment if you buy a property with positive cash flow. Real estate investing can provide a tax break for depreciation. It also is a great learning opportunity for your children as it can teach them critical concepts related to real estate and financing such as mortgages, interest rates, depreciation, amortization, and how to manage a property. However, contrary to a 529 account, a real estate investment will not grow tax-free and is not as liquid. There are also costs associated with selling or refinancing real estate property, which does not apply with a 529.

Using real estate exclusively to save for college, or combining a real estate strategy with another strategy, such as having a 529 account, is an option to explore.

Pros:

- Depreciation tax break
- Learning opportunity
- Long-term passive income opportunity
- Tenant(s) pay off.

Cons:

- Not liquid
- Will not grow tax-free
- Selling and refinancing fees
- High upfront investment (down payment).

Reducing education expense

As your child gets closer to the time they are expected to begin their postsecondary education, you should encourage them to explore opportunities to reduce the cost of their postsecondary education. Whether it is college or vocational school, it is worth researching alternative ways to finance their education.

If you can reduce the cost of college, the money left over in the college savings account can be used elsewhere. For instance, if your oldest child is the beneficiary of a scholarship, you can change the beneficiary on a 529 plan to a sibling, and use the funds for the sibling's college expenses. If you only have one child and they receive a full-ride scholarship, you can pay the federal taxes on the gains and use the money elsewhere. Part of the money can be used to help your child fund an investment account or contribute to a down payment on their first property. Here are six common ways to explore to reduce the cost of post secondary education when the time comes.

1. Scholarships

Each year, in the United States, approximately 46 billion dollars of scholarships and grants are awarded by colleges, universities, and the U.S. Department of Education.[v] There are many types of scholarships available to help pay for college. Sometime around freshman year, it would be wise for your child to start researching scholarships that he/she could qualify for and become familiar with application requirements. The most common scholarships are based on the categories below.

Academic scholarships

Academic scholarships are for high-performing students, usually awarded by universities or private organizations. These scholarships are for our young Kings and Queens who are at the top of their class. Most of these merit-based scholarships will partially fund college for the recipient, while others will cover the total cost of attending college.

Athletic scholarships

Athletic scholarships are for students who are talented in a specific sport. As of 2019, the average athletic scholarship in the United States was 18,000 dollars a year per student-athlete.[vi]

Personal background scholarships
Personal background scholarships are to attract students who are usually underrepresented. These scholarships are based on various personal, social, or demographic factors. These factors include, but are not limited to, race, gender, sexual orientation, religion, family associations, military status, and place of origin.

Community service scholarships
Community service scholarships are awarded to students for actively participating in their community by volunteering.

Financial need scholarships
Need-based scholarships are for students from low-income families. These scholarships are typically school sponsored or privately funded and require filling out a Free Application for Federal Student Aid (FAFSA).

Career-specific scholarships
Career-specific scholarships are granted to students who are planning to pursue a specific career. These scholarships are more common in areas of study that are underrepresented, such as engineering or nursing.

Unique talents or traits scholarships
Unique talent or trait scholarships award students particularly gifted in a specific area, from visual arts to writing. If your child has a specific talent or ability, there might be a scholarship for them.

There are hundreds of thousands of scholarships available to high school seniors to attend college every year. The odds of obtaining a full-ride scholarship are slim if a child is not academically in the top 1 percent or a high-performing athlete. However, the chances of getting a partial scholarship are pretty high—at 50 percent. For the year 2018–2019, the average scholarship or grant for an undergraduate student was 9,520 dollars.[VII] This amount can also increase if your child receives more than one scholarship. For that reason, scholarship applications should be taken very seriously. Your child should be just as diligent at searching for scholarships and writing essays, as they would be at working a job. The reward of reducing the cost to attend college can have a significant impact on their long-term financials.

There are many tools to help you with your scholarship search. One of those tools is Scholly. Scholly is an application founded by Christopher Gray, a Black teenager who won 1.3 million dollars in scholarship money to attend college. The Scholly search engine matches students with a list of scholarships relevant to them based on the profile they fill out.

2. Grants

Grants are usually awarded by federal assistance programs, schools, and organizations based on financial need. Similar to a scholarship, it is free money that you do not have to reimburse.

Pell grants are the United States' largest financial need-based grant program, funded by the Department of Education. To qualify to receive a Pell Grant, you need to fill out a FAFSA application.

3. Take college credits while in high school

Taking college credits before beginning college is another way to reduce the cost of college. Many high school students are eligible to take Advancement Placement (AP) courses to get college credit. This alternative is considerably cheaper than taking the class as a college student. It can help reduce the cost of college and serve as preparation for college-level education.

4. Start at a community college

To reduce the cost of attending college, young adults can also start at a community college and transfer to a four-year university after the first two years. Starting at community college can significantly reduce the cost of college—it can sometimes be more than half the cost of four-year-universities. What matters most is the school you graduated from, not the school where you started your education. It is an alternative to explore as you look for a way to reduce the cost of college. Starting at a community college is also a great option if your child considers other post secondary options such as trade school.

5. Live at home

Living at home is an option to consider if your child decides to attend a college close to home. If you are concerned about your child not getting the full college experience, it is an option for them to stay on campus the first year and live at home for the remainder of their degree. Living at home will save a lot of money on housing expenses.

Building wealth through the stock market

Two common misconceptions about wealth building are that to become a millionaire, a person needs to either save a million dollars or have a six-figure income. It is wise to have discussions with our young adults—to help them understand that the key to building wealth and becoming a millionaire is to start saving and investing early to take advantage of compound interest. With compound interest, becoming a millionaire is possible even on a five-figure salary.

Let us say that you gift your twenty-two-year-old with 1,000 dollars as a graduation present to put in a retirement account. The condition is that they do not touch the money until retirement. If they continue to save 500 dollars a month (6,000 dollars a year) for the next thirty-seven years, at fifty-nine years old, they will have over a million dollars, assuming a reasonable rate of return of 7 percent.

Balances by age (in $)

Age	Beginning	Investment Growth	Contributions	Retirement Balance
22	1,000	70	6,000	7,070
25	20,514	1,436	6,000	27,950
30	63,277	4,429	6,000	73,706
35	123,254	8,628	6,000	137,881
40	207,374	14,516	6,000	227,890
45	325,357	22,775	6,000	354,132
50	490,835	34,358	6,000	531,193
55	722,926	50,605	6,000	779,531
59	974,248	68,197	6,000	1,048,445
60	1,048,245	73,391	6,000	1,127,837

If they were to start ten years later at age thirty-two, they would need to save 1,000 dollars a month for thirty-eight years to get to a million dollars by age sixty.

Balances by age (in $)

Age	Beginning	Investment Growth	Contributions	Retirement Balance
32	1,000	70	12,000	7,070
35	39,804	2,786	12,000	54,590
40	124,836	8,739	12,000	145,574
45	244,098	17,087	12,000	273,184
50	411,368	28,796	12,000	452,164
55	645,974	45,218	12,000	703,192
59	900,020	63,001	12,000	975,021
60	975,021	68,251	12,000	1,055,273

These two examples illustrate how, when you start early, you do not have to save as much; and that a six-figure income is not necessary to get to a million dollars.

Helping our Kings and Queens open their minds and understand that they can have a million dollars or more in investments at retirement—if they start early, save, and invest consistently—is essential. A million dollars will likely not be enough by the time they retire, but most importantly, understanding that with discipline, the first million dollars is within reach will help shape their mindset. It can serve as motivation to start saving early, work harder, and learn more about personal finance—which will lead to even more success.

Most millionaires save at least 20 percent of their income toward retirement, according to Fidelity. It is another piece of valuable information to share with our children. The sooner they understand that the higher percentage of their income they save and invest, the better off they will be in the long run.

Basic investment guidelines.

Here are four guidelines to keep in mind to minimize risk when investing in the stock market.

- Invest money that you will not need in the near future
- Diversify your portfolio
- Do not try to beat the market
- Maximize your returns by using tax-advantaged accounts.

1. Invest money that you will not need in the near future

The stock market is volatile. Keeping your emergency fund or any money that you will need in the next five to seven years in the stock market is risky. The stock market is unpredictable and could significantly drop when you plan to take your money out. It is much wiser to invest with a long-term strategy in mind to maximize returns.

2. Diversify your portfolio

It is best to own a diversified portfolio to lower your risk. However, stock picking is not for everyone. As a rule of thumb, a well-balanced stock portfolio should have twenty to thirty stocks. Stock prices can be very volatile, and picking the right stocks is similar to a gamble for inexperienced investors. A better alternative is to use exchange-traded funds or low-cost mutual funds, which hold stocks, bonds, assets, and other financial securities. With this option, you can have a well-diversified portfolio with only a few funds, depending on the funds you pick. However, a healthy investment portfolio should not only be diversified across companies, but also across industries.

3. Do not try to beat the market
Buying and selling stocks based on market volatility is a risky strategy. History has shown that unless you are a professional day trader, that strategy does not work, especially in the long run. If you are an inexperienced investor, it is best to focus on long-term investing. Risking your retirement savings by trying to beat the market is not a good idea. A much better alternative is to start investing early and long-term to make average returns.

4. Maximize your returns by using tax-advantaged accounts
When investing money, you should invest in tax-advantaged accounts like 401(k) and Roth IRAs for the tax benefits before investing in traditional accounts. See the Retirement section of the book for additional details.

Actively-managed funds versus passively-managed funds

Actively-managed index funds are often pushed upon investors. However, if you are paying more than 1 percent in expense ratio, consider a less expensive fund. Fund managers rarely ever beat the market. They tend to be costly, which will significantly impact your long-term returns. If you find a fund manager who has beaten the market in the past, there is no guarantee that they will continue to beat the market in the future. It is rarely worth the risk to pay a high expense ratio, so you should keep that in mind before selecting an actively managed-index fund.

Asset allocation by age

Asset allocation is an investment strategy aiming to balance risk and reward based on an investor's age. Asset allocation breaks down your investment portfolio based on stocks and fixed-income investments like bonds.

A common rule of thumb to determine what your asset allocation should be by age is the formula to calculate the percentage of your portfolio that should be in stocks, which is 100 minus age.

If you are thirty years old, the calculation is as follows: 100 − 30 = 70

At thirty years, according to this rule of thumb, 70 percent of your portfolio should be in stocks, while the remaining 30 percent should be in fixed-income investments. Every year, your investment portfolio should be adjusted to match your age.

With the increasing life expectancy, the 110 rule of thumb has gained popularity—110 minus age equals percentage of the portfolio in stocks.

If you are thirty years old, the calculation is as follows: 110 − 30 = 80

At thirty, according to this rule of thumb, 80 percent of your portfolio should be in stocks, while the remaining 20 percent should be in fixed-income investments. Every year, your investment portfolio should be adjusted to match your age.

The choice between the first and second method depends on your risk tolerance level. The second method is riskier but is likely to give you higher returns—as long as you remember to focus on a long-term investment strategy. It is essential to review your asset allocation every year to make sure that it is appropriate based on your age.

Equity investments
1. Stocks

The best way to get started in the stock market is to invest in a total stock market exchange traded-funds like the Vanguard Total Stock Market ETF (VTI), for example. VTI holds three thousand six hundred small, mid, and large-capitalization U.S. company stocks. It is a passively managed fund with a low expense ratio of 0.03 percent. There are other total stock market index funds options that are equally as good as Vanguard's VTI. A Vanguard index-fund might be more attractive because of the unique way Vanguard is structured. Investment companies typically aim to keep both their investors and their owners happy. For example, T. Rowe Price is a publicly-traded company; in addition to pleasing its customers, it must also please stockholders. Fidelity is a privately owned company, which means that it must serve the interest of its owners. However, Vanguard is owned by its customers, and it operates at cost. For that reason, Vanguard has an extra incentive to keep its costs low—and make investors/owners happy—that most other brokerage firms do not.

At your brokerage account, you can research the total stock market fund option with the lowest expense ratio that you can purchase without incurring any fees.

When you first start investing, you could exclusively invest in that type of fund for the equity allocation of your portfolio. If you are comfortable with purchasing international stocks, you could invest 80 to 85 percent of your stock portfolio in a US total market index fund, and the remaining 15 to 20 percent in an international index fund or ETF.

The iShares Core MSCI EAFE is a low-cost ETF holding small, mid- and large-capitalization European, Australian, Asian, and Far East company stocks. iShares Core MSCI EAFE is a passively managed fund with an expense ratio of 0.07 percent. You can also look for similar funds with a lower expense ratio. As a rule of thumb, a reasonable expense ratio is less than 1 percent for actively managed funds, and below 0.3 percent for passively managed funds.

Though the iShares Core MSCI EAFE expense ratio is higher than the VTI expense ratio, it is within a reasonable range.

For every one thousand dollars invested, VTI would cost you 30 cents a year, while iShares Core MSCI EAFE would cost 70 cents a year.

For instance, let us consider an investment of 70,000 dollars of your portfolio in iShares Core MSCI EAFE, and let us assume a 7 percent return (4,900 dollars) in the first year. It would cost you about 52 dollars the first year, as opposed to 22 dollars with VTI. However, the slightly higher fee (30 dollars) would give you more international exposure.

Dollar-cost averaging

When investing in total stock market investment funds, a good strategy to consider is dollar-cost averaging. This strategy consists in making investment purchases at regular intervals in equal amounts, as opposed to investing large sums of money at once. Dollar-cost averaging is a good way to lower risk. When you invest your money all at once, you risk buying at a peak—which can then be followed by a price drop. When dollar-cost averaging, you lower the risk by spreading out your investment over time.

Value averaging

Value averaging is a strategy consisting in buying more shares when the share price falls and fewer shares when the price increases. As opposed to dollar-cost averaging, value averaging does not involve purchasing a set amount of shares each period. It requires determining your value path, which is the value you want your portfolio to reach by a specific time, and then working backward to determine how much your portfolio will need to grow each period to achieve your objective.

Let us assume that you want your portfolio to grow by 2,000 dollars every year. At the beginning of the year, you invest 2,000 dollars.

Let us say that your portfolio is worth 2,500 dollars after market returns at the end of the first year.

Based on your value path, your portfolio should be worth 4,000 dollars at the beginning of the following year. As such, at the beginning of year two, you will invest 1,500 dollars instead of 2,000 dollars. This 1,500 represents the difference between your 4,000 value path and the 2,500 dollar value at year-end.

Value averaging requires a lot more work than dollar-cost averaging. It is an alternative to consider for more experienced investors.

As you become more knowledgeable about the stock market, you might become more interested in picking individual stocks.

Core-satellite investing

The core-satellite investing strategy consists of having the majority of your portfolio in passive investments, such as total stock market index funds, and the remainder of your portfolio in actively managed funds or individual stocks.

The passive section of your portfolio is the core. It makes up the majority of your holdings and is the less risky part of your portfolio. Over time, you should continue to add to the core and let it grow.

The active section of your portfolio is the satellite, which is significantly smaller than the core. In the satellite section of your portfolio, you take more risks and actively trade to outperform the market. Over time, you will continue to add to and actively trade investments in your portfolio's satellite section. For this part of your portfolio, you can select sector-specific funds, as long as you continue to diversify across different industries.

A good rule of thumb to consider under this strategy for your asset allocation is 80 percent or more for the core, and 20 percent or less for the satellite. As you get closer to retirement, consider reducing your portfolio's satellite portion compared to the core.

Value investing

The value investing strategy consists in purchasing stocks that you believe to be undervalued. Value investors look to buy shares of stocks they deem to be discounted, with plans to keep them long-term. Value investing is for the more savvy investor. Under this strategy, a valuable tool is the price-to-earnings ratio (P/E). To calculate the P/E ratio, divide the stock's share price by its earnings per share (EPS). The P/E ratio gives you an idea of how much you are paying per dollar of earnings, and whether the stock price is low or high compared to other companies in the sector. Value investors are more interested in stocks with lower P/E ratios.

If stock X is trading for 100 dollars per share, with an EPS of 4 dollars, its P/E ratio is 100 divided by 4, or 25. P/E ratios vary by industry and are also affected by the world's current events. It is a good tool to compare industries, as well as companies. But, a lower P/E ratio does not mean you should buy the stock. It is a starting point to narrow down a list of stocks to further research.

Fixed-income investments

Fixed-income investments pay a set return on your investment based on a predetermined schedule. The most common fixed-income investments are bonds, certificates of deposits, and money market funds.

Bonds

Bonds are fixed-income instruments under which the bond issuer owes the bond holder a debt, commits to paying back the principal at the maturity date, and pays interest at fixed dates.

The government or corporations issue individual bonds for a specific period, typically ranging from one year to thirty years. It is wise to focus on bonds with terms of three years or less. Interest rates fluctuate, and market circumstances change, so locking in a shorter-term rate mitigate the risk of missing out on future higher bond interest rates or investment opportunities. Bond funds typically hold a large number of individual bonds with various maturity dates and coupon rates. As such, they provide more diversification. However, unlike with individual funds, there is no guarantee with bond funds that you will get your investment back.

Certificates of Deposit

A certificate of deposit (CD) is a financial product that provides an interest rate premium to customers. The premium is in exchange for the customer's agreement to leave a set sum of money in the CD untouched for a predetermined period. Unlike a savings account that allows customers to withdraw their money without penalties, certificates of deposits charge early withdrawal penalties. For that reason, certificates of deposit provide higher interest rates than saving accounts.

Money market accounts

A money market account is a savings account with some features of a checking account. Typically, money market accounts offer higher interest rates than regular savings accounts. They also have a higher minimum deposit or balance requirement than savings accounts. Money market accounts are more accessible than CDs as they typically do not charge penalties for making up to certain number of withdrawals every month.

Retirement accounts vs. brokerage accounts

Financial investments are a great way to build wealth. Using tax advantaged accounts will help you save money, which can, in turn, increase your returns. Focusing your energy on accounts providing tax benefits first, before looking into standard brokerage accounts, is a smart thing to do.

A standard brokerage account provides access to a broader selection of stocks, mutual funds, bonds, and exchange-traded funds than most retirement accounts. But any investment gains are subject to taxes the year that they are realized, regardless of whether the money is withdrawn from the account. For savvy investors, this type of account is used to take more risk with your investment strategy to obtain potentially higher future rewards. However, retirement saving and investing should be the priority.

Building wealth through real estate

In the past two hundred years, the vast majority of millionaires in the United States have used real estate as a tool for wealth building.

According to a report published by Coldwell Banker, an American real estate franchise with three thousand offices around the world, there were 618,000 millionaires between the ages of twenty-three and thirty-seven in America.[VIII] Of those millennial millionaires, 92 percent were homeowners, owning an average of three properties, with a real estate portfolio worth 1.4 million dollars.

Real estate is the most common path to wealth. However, not every property will turn into a good investment. We should educate ourselves about real estate and prepare our Kings and Queens to take advantage of this wealth-building strategy.

Understanding the intricacies of real estate, including how it can generate wealth, and how to evaluate a potential investment property, is crucial to using real estate to build wealth effectively.

There are four main ways real estate can generate wealth: cash flow, tax benefits, loan amortization, and appreciation.

Cash flow

Cash flow is the money that you take home after covering your property expenses as a real estate investor. A common mistake made by new investors is only to consider the obvious costs, such as mortgage, taxes, and utilities, if applicable. However, other costs like regular maintenance and repairs, vacancy—the time a property can be expected to be vacant, or capital expenditures—expensive one-time expenses such as replacing a roof or appliances, should also be included in the property expenses.

Let us pretend that you own the property below.

Purchase price: $160,000
Rent: $1,750
Recurring annual expenses: $1,681

Mortgage principal and interest: $12,144
Taxes and insurance: $2,248
Regular maintenance and repairs: $2,000
Total recurring expenses: $18,432 annually or $1,536 monthly.

Most common capital expenditures:
Water heater (every 10 years): $600/10 = $60
Roof (every 25 years): $5,000/ 25 = $200
Appliances (every 10 years): $1,000/10 = $100
Plumbing (every 30 years): $3,000/30 = $100
HVAC unit (every 10 years): $3,000/10 = $30

Flooring (every 6 years): $3,000/6 = $500
Paint (every 5 years): $2,500/5 =$500
Counters and cabinets (every 20 years): $3,000/20 = $150
Landscaping (every 10 years): $1,000/10 = $100
Total capital expenditures: $1,740 annually or $145 monthly

Cash Flow = 1,750 − (1,536 + 145) = 69 dollars monthly or 828 dollars annually.

Tax benefits

Tax benefits are the tax advantages resulting from owning real estate. Real estate tax benefits will vary depending on where you live. In the United States, the most common real estate tax benefits are tax deductions, depreciation, and capital gain taxes (as opposed to higher income taxes), tax-deferred or tax-free investments, passive income, and opportunity zone investments.

Tax deductions give you the ability to deduct expenses related to your investment property, such as property taxes and insurance, mortgage interest, property repairs, and advertising expenses.

Depreciation allows you to write off the cost of an income-producing property, or of a property with a business use over time—twenty-seven-and-a-half years for residential properties, and thirty-nine years for commercial properties in 2020. Depreciation accounts for a decrease in value resulting from the usage and wear and tear of the property, which helps reduce your tax burden.

If you purchased a single-family rental property for 150,000 dollars, you would be able to deduct 5,455 dollars annually for twenty-seven-and-a-half years as long as you continue to own the investment property during that period. You could also deduct certain expenses to improve the property over that period, such as capital expenditures.

Capital gains are the profits you receive from selling an asset, such as real estate property or stocks. Capital gain taxes are paid on income resulting from the sale. Capital gain taxes on long-term investments, investments held for a year or longer, tend to be lower than ordinary income taxes.

There are also tax-deferred and tax-free advantages with real estate. With a 1031 exchange, a real estate investor can defer capital gain taxes on an investment property. By completing the purchase of another qualifying property within a specific time window after the sale, hundred and eighty days as of 2020, capital gain taxes can be deferred.

Several individual retirement accounts such as solo 401(k)s, SEP IRAs, or self-directed IRAs, as well as a health savings accounts (HSAs), allow investments in alternative real estate assets, tax-free or tax-deferred—under specific contribution limits and requirements.

Under the home sales tax exclusion, a person can exclude up to a certain amount of capital gains from the sale of their primary residence as long as they meet specific criteria. To qualify for the home sales tax exclusion, you must own the home and have used it as your principal residence for at least two years out of the five years before the sale date.

As of 2020, you could exclude up to 250,000 dollars as an individual, and 500,000 dollars as a couple filing a joint tax return.

Franck and Stacy, a married couple, purchased a house for 150,000 dollars in 2008. After living in the house for eight years, they decided to sell it for 250,000 dollars. Frank and Stacy made capital gains of 100,000 dollars on the sale. However, they did not owe any taxes under the home sales tax exclusion, because a 100,000 dollars gain is below the 500,000 dollars exclusion.

Passive income is income derived from an investment without active participation. Rental income typically qualifies as passive income. Passive income is taxed at a lower rate as it is not subject to Social Security and Medicare taxes.

Under the Tax Cut and Jobs Act of 2017, the United States has identified specific areas called "opportunity zones," for which the government provides tax incentives. Opportunity zones are usually in low-income communities. They provide investors with an opportunity to fund projects in economically distressed neighborhoods and help build those neighborhoods. Opportunity zones present an excellent chance for Black investors to build wealth in real estate and transform their communities.

Loan pay-down

When you purchase an investment property with a mortgage and every time you make a mortgage payment, your loan balance decreases. When your loan balance decreases, your equity in the home increases.

If your property has positive cash flow or zero cash flow, your tenant will pay-down the loan for you over time.

In 2012, Nia put a 26,000 dollars down payment on a 130,000 dollars investment property. On average, the property has produced a positive cash flow of 1,200 dollars a year. For the remaining twenty-two years of the mortgage, even if the property did not produce any cash flow and did not increase in value, Nia would have a 130,000 dollars property paid off in majority by her tenant(s).

Appreciation

Real estate appreciation is when the value of a property increases. Over time, real estate prices fluctuate. Sometimes properties even lose value, but in the long run, the value of most real estate properties increases. Often, appreciation is the result of market growth, but real estate appreciation can also be forced through property improvements—forced equity.

In the previous example, Nia purchased the property for 130,000 dollars in 2012. In early 2020, the property was valued at 170,000 dollars, appreciating by 30.8 percent in eight years.

In 2019, James, a real estate investor, purchased a fixer-upper property in pretty bad shape for 73,000 dollars. He invested another 120,000 dollars in fixing up the property and force appreciation—which brought his total investment to 193,000 dollars. A few months later, James sold the property for 315,000 dollars.

The most common real estate strategies

There are many real estate strategies, but this book focuses on eight common strategies—house hacking, live-in-then-rent, live-in-flip, BRRR strategy, buy-and-hold rental, fix-and-flip, wholesaling, and real estate investing trusts.

House hacking is when you live in a home that also produces income. Properties used for house hacking can be multifamily homes like a duplex, triplex, fourplex, or a house with an extra space that can be rented—like a basement or spare bedroom or guest house. House hacking helps reduce or even eliminate your main housing expenses. It is also a great introduction to being a landlord. The down payment requirement on a house hack is lower than on an investment property because it is also your primary residence. When you are ready to purchase another property, you can move out and convert that property into a long-term rental.

Live-in-then-rent is when you live in a house and then convert it to a rental. Under the live-in-then rent strategy, you purchase the property as your main residence. As such, similar to house hacking, the down payment requirement is lower. However, the property must be a good fit as your main residence, and as a rental property when you decide to move out. The main difference between the house hacking strategy and the live-in-then-rent strategy is that you do not live in the house while renting it.

Live-in-flip is when you buy a property under market value, with the intent to move in renovate it and sell at a profit. A live-in-flip is a primary residence; thus, you can purchase the property with a lower down payment. Typically, most people live in a house for at least two years before reselling it, to take advantage of the home sales tax exclusion (250,000 dollars for an individual and 500,000 dollars for a couple filing jointly in 2020). Living in a house while renovating it can be challenging. But, many investors have used this strategy repeatedly to build wealth.

BRRRR investing stands for Buy-Remodel-Rent-Refinance-Repeat. Under the BRRRR strategy, you look for fixer-upper properties to purchase under market value, usually with short-term financing. Once you fix the property and stabilize it, you then refinance it with a long-term mortgage. At that point, you have forced equity in the property. You can decide to pull some money out when refinancing and repeat this strategy with another property that you buy under market value with the intent to fix.

Buy-and-hold rental is when you purchase a property intending to hold it long-term. This strategy provides benefits such as rental income, long-term price appreciation, and tax breaks from depreciation expenses. Buy-and-hold rental is a strategy to consider, particularly in good locations with growth potential. It is important to note that you will be subject to taxes under this strategy if you decide to sell the property.

Fix-and-flip is when you buy a property that needs repair with the intent to fix it up and sell it back for profit. The main difference with the live-in-flip is that you do not live in the property. As such, you will not be able to take advantage of tax breaks or lower down payment option. This strategy requires actively participating in overseeing the project to ensure the timeline is respected. But it is attractive to investors looking for a short-term way to generate cash for future investments.

Wholesaling is the process of getting a house under market value under contract, to then assign it to a buyer. Wholesaling is one of the strategies requiring the least amount of financial investment. Your investment is essentially the amount that you put under escrow to get the house under contract and the time that you spend finding a buyer. The amount you put in escrow should not be more than 1 or 2 percent of the purchase price—between 1,500 and 3,000 dollars for a 150,000 dollars home. With this strategy, you will have to work hard under tight deadlines as a salesperson to find a buyer, who is typically an investor, so that you can receive an assignment fee. You will also have to pay taxes on your earnings. Wholesaling is a good way for beginners to learn about real estate and make good money without spending too much of their own money.

Real Estate Investing Trusts (REITs)

Real Estate Investing Trusts is one of the most passive investing strategies in real estate. Purchasing real estate investment trusts is similar to buying mutual funds. With a REIT investment, you own shares of income-producing real estate properties. This strategy offers the opportunity to make high returns, but as owning REITs is similar to investing in stocks, there is a lot of volatility and can result in taxes based on the type of investment account you have. Refer to the "Traditional Retirement" section of the book for more details.

One of my acquaintances, Linda, owned four rental properties, but she had a negative cash flow because her rents did not fully cover her mortgage, taxes, and other expenses. In 2008, when the housing market crashed, Linda was making 60,000 dollars a year at her job, and she had 500,000 dollars of mortgage debt and three vacant units. Linda ended up losing all four properties to short sales. Over the next couple of years, Linda increased her salary to 95,000 dollars. She decided to live a more frugal lifestyle, rent a small apartment for 800 dollars a month, and save as much money as possible. Five years later, Linda found a fixer-upper property that she purchased for 75,000 dollars in cash. Linda moved into the property, spent 20,000 dollars to renovate it, and sold it for 125,000 dollars. Linda made a profit of 30,000 dollars and later purchased a buy-and-hold property with the profit. She also bought a live-in-flip property in cash. Linda now owns two real estate investment properties, with one paid off. She learned her lessons on overleveraging debt and favors a more conservative approach.

Real estate is a great way to build wealth. But it is essential not to only focus on the potential rewards. It is crucial to take the time to learn about the business to create long-term real estate wealth. Educate yourself and your children on the potential for wealth building that real estate provides. Learn how to assess the risks and quality of a real estate investment. Failing to do so can result in growing your portfolio too fast because of overleveraging debt, not having enough cash reserves on hand to prepare for rainy days, and risk losing everything in a downturn. Understanding real estate, knowing how to evaluate investments, having the appropriate cash reserves, and focusing on a steady growth is what you should teach your kids to create generational wealth.

CHAPTER 11
Work Ethic and Entrepreneurship

Teaching children the value of hard work

My first introduction to the workforce was in middle school. Every Wednesday afternoon, I diligently answered calls at my mother's office and welcomed patients into the office. As my mother and father's office buildings were next to each other, I also spent time at my father's office, pretending to be his secretary. The time I spent at my parents' offices at a young age allowed me to see how hard my parents worked and exposed me to entrepreneurship.

Then, one summer, I asked my dad if I could help at his small cosmetics manufacturing plant. My father agreed to let me spend time at the plant a couple of days a week. My responsibility was far from glamourous. It consisted of pushing a button to put moisturizing cream in a container before passing it down the assembly line. I worked at the manufacturing plant by choice, and that experience was eye-opening for me.

I first fell in love with entrepreneurship in my early college years. Back then, my family and friends used to call me "lady hustle" because I was always looking for ways to make money.

During my college years, I used to buy cellphones and other electronics in bulk in China and resell them on the internet. I purchased and resold concert tickets. I also developed an interest in the stock market and started day trading. Then, my soon-to-be husband and I started making and selling T-shirts.

I believe that the experiences I had as a youth contributed to developing the drive necessary to build multiple streams of income. My interests guided my decisions to explore various avenues for generating revenue. When I turned sixteen, I decided to take a summer job as a cashier. I did not have any specific needs at the time, but I wanted to make my own money. At the end of that summer, I was very proud to buy presents for my parents with my hard-earned money, and show my mother how good a saver I was. These two experiences shaped me. They helped me understand the value of money and develop a strong work ethic.

A critical element to building wealth is figuring out avenues to increase your income. When you have a salary, you are typically limited by how much money you can make. But, when you are an entrepreneur, there is no limit to your earning potential.

According to the Global Entrepreneurship and Development Index (GEDI), which reviews entrepreneurial factors in different countries and compares them against social and economic infrastructure, the United States is the best environment in the world to cultivate entrepreneurs.[i]

A Black business owner has, on average, a net worth twelve times higher than that of a Black person who does not own a business.[ii] Black entrepreneurs support their families with their businesses, but they also support the Black community. Black companies are the second-highest employers of Black people after the government. There are four million minority-owned businesses in the United States, and those businesses generate annual sales of 700 billion dollars.[iii]

Minority businesses also account for more than half of the two million new businesses in the United States in the past ten years.

There are over two million businesses in the United States owned by Black people,[iv] with many of them in advertising, auto dealerships, consulting services, restaurants, barbershops, and beauty salons.

Worldwide Technology, a global technology consulting firm, is the largest Black-owned business in the country, generating twelve billion dollars of annual revenue.

Though these numbers are encouraging, there is room for more representation of Black people in entrepreneurship. While Black people make up 14 percent of the US population, we represent less than 8 percent of the country's businesses.

Starting a business can be a great way to increase your income and generate wealth, but entrepreneurship is not for everyone. Being an entrepreneur comes with additional risks and responsibilities. It also requires more effort, resilience, and creativity to start and grow your business. However, most successful entrepreneurs report being more fulfilled and motivated to work than when they were corporate employees. Entrepreneurship is an avenue to consider for anyone willing to work hard to remove the income ceiling in their lives.

My husband's friend Salim is the son of a mechanical engineer, Sam, who migrated to the United States forty years ago in pursuit of a better life. After working in the corporate world for ten years, Sam opened a mechanic shop. He had four boys who all worked in the family business as teenagers. Two of Sam's sons, Kareem and Salim, took over the company's reign while they were in college. They expanded the company to provide car audio services to its customers and considerably grew the business. Kareem and Salim then expanded the family business by getting involved in other successful retail ventures. While their two brothers decided to pursue other entrepreneurial endeavors, all four kids have successful businesses. They all credit their professional path to being exposed to and seeing the benefits of entrepreneurship at a young age.

As parents, we should pay close attention to what appears to be of interest to our children and what they seem to be passionate about. Our children might not be interested in entrepreneurship at a young age, but we can always have discussions to pique their interest. As they grow up, we should support them to generate income from their interests.

My six-year-old Cecilia has shown a lot of interest in designing her T-shirts since she saw me wear an old T-shirt I had designed back in college. Cecilia was very curious to learn about the process I went through to design the shirt. At the time, she asked me if she could design her own. As Cecilia is very much into arts and crafts and creating a T-shirt has been a recurring interest, my husband and I intend to introduce her to entrepreneurship that way. We have discussed with Cecilia that she will be responsible for conceptualizing a few T-shirts with her little sisters. My husband and I then plan to show her how we list the T-shirts on the internet to sell them. We have discussed a small initial investment for this project. Cecilia will also put five dollars toward the project to move forward. Her five-dollar investment is to help ensure she has a vested interest in the venture's success. As we embark on this project, we will introduce Cecilia to the concepts of sales price, margins, and marketing. Whether this venture is profitable or not, Cecilia will gain exposure to entrepreneurship and learn key lessons about money.

Many people plan to work for an employer for a few years before starting their own business. However, over time, people's situations change, and the opportunity cost to pursue entrepreneurship increases. Most people get married or start families, and their risk tolerance decreases as their need for financial security increases. If our kids have an interest in owning their own business, we can encourage them to focus on that early on in life, when their opportunity cost is lower.

Young entrepreneurs typically have more time early in their careers to devote to their business than older adults with family responsibilities. It might be an option, for kids who are considering starting their own business, to have a full-time corporate job while building their business. But, if they are interested in focusing on entrepreneurship early on, it is an option to explore. Young adults are more inclined to live with roommates and survive on a lean budget to reduce their expenses. As creative young adults with the strong work ethic you would have instilled in them, young entrepreneurs are more likely to challenge the status quo and be well-positioned for success.

CHAPTER 12
Building Multiple Sources of Income

Increasing your income streams

I graduated from college during the Great Recession of 2007. I also witnessed the economic downturn resulting from the worldwide COVID-19 outbreak in early 2020.

In both instances, millions of people lost their jobs overnight. What I quickly understood is that job security does not exist. It was another reminder of the importance of building multiple streams of income. Additional sources of income can provide financial protection in case of a job or income loss. In addition to providing a safety net, having a secondary source of income allows you to fund other projects when your primary income source covers your living expenses. Having a side hustle outside of a regular job is a great way to build a business slowly.

There are two kinds of income: passive and active.

Active income is earned by working diligently to receive the income. Passive income is earned with little to no effort. Passive income is what you should focus your long-term plans on to build long-term wealth.

Active income
- Business profits
- Wages
- Tips

Salaries
Commissions.

Passive Income
Rental income
Dividends
Interest income
Royalties
Capital gains from assets sale.

Thomas Corley studied the habits of millionaires for five years. Based on his study, 65 percent of self-made millionaires in the United States of America had three streams of income, 45 percent had four streams of income, and 29 percent had five or more streams of income.[1]

According to the Internal Revenue Service, the most common income streams for millionaires in the United States are:

Earned income from a paycheck
Profits from businesses they own
Rental income from real estate
Dividends from stocks
Interest income
Royalties from selling rights to something they invented or wrote
Capital gains from selling appreciating assets.

Raising our kids to understand the importance of having multiple streams of income is crucial to building generational wealth. When you have several revenue streams, when one stream suffers, you can weather the storm with the other income stream(s) that you already have.

CHAPTER 13
Estate Planning
Organizing your affairs for your loved ones

In the early 2000s, a young actor suddenly died, leaving behind his minor daughter and his partner, who was the child's mother. He had not updated his will after having a child, so his entire estate went to his parents and siblings, leaving nothing to his daughter or partner. The late actor's family decided to donate most of his estate to his daughter. Though this is a beautiful story of love and integrity demonstrated by the actor's family, the story typically does not end on such a positive note when there is money involved. Poor estate planning often results in legal battles and a mountain of legal fees.

Close to two decades ago, a famous entertainer died, leaving behind a sizable estate. He had multiple children and a wife that he had been separated from for many years—but they never legally divorced. At the time of his death, he had been living with his girlfriend for many years. However, he never updated his will after separating from his wife. His entire estate went to his ex-wife, while the children and his partner did not inherit anything. More than a decade after his death, the family was still fighting over his estate.

Even though these two examples are of wealthy celebrities, proper estate planning is equally as important when you are not rich. Estate planning is what you do to prepare your loved ones for life after your death. A common misconception is that only rich people should worry about estate planning. However, estate planning is not limited to the organization of your finances. It also encompasses who should raise your minor children if you are no longer there, who you trust to handle your affairs should you become incapacitated, and any other instructions you may have for your loved ones.

As a parent, a spouse, or anyone with dependents, it is essential to have your estate plans in order—no matter your age.

Most people do not want to think about their mortality; however, death is a guaranteed part of life.

If you do not get your affairs in order, you leave the state or country to make the decisions. Dealing with the court system is usually slow and is likely to cause stress on loved ones and a financial burden. You should think of estate planning as the last gift to your dependents and loved ones. Having your affairs in order will help avoid unnecessary stress on top of the pain and turmoil they will experience as a result of losing you.

This chapter addresses essential documents for estate planning. However, laws and regulations change based on state and country. It is crucial to research the laws and regulations that apply to your state or country. It would also be wise to work with an attorney to ensure that the documents you use for your estate planning are legal and will be enforceable when the time comes.

Will or testament

A will is a legal document expressing your final wishes. It should cover your decisions regarding your children's care and designate your minor children's legal guardian(s), and executor or your will. In your testament, you can also address any last wishes you have, including funeral arrangements. If you have financial assets, your testament should also cover how you would like your assets to be distributed upon your death and provide a list of the significant assets you may have. Your state or country may have minimum requirements regarding assets distribution, which is another reason it is wise to work with a professional to ensure your will is enforceable.

I wrote my first will when I got married in my mid-twenties. I typed the document myself, printed it, and signed it. For the next two years, I had no idea that my will had no legal standing.

It was not until my first child was born that I realized that my testament was invalid. I learned then that two witnesses must be present when you sign a will in the state where I reside.

After doing further research on estate planning, I discovered that having a will was insufficient. Minor children who are beneficiaries cannot legally manage assets until they reach the age of majority. In the event the worse were to happen to my husband and me, we needed a couple more documents to ensure our child would be adequately taken care of.

In the state of Georgia, when you only rely on a will for your estate planning, the process must go through probate court. It can take years and can be costly if contested. If we did not get our affairs in order, our daughter being a minor, the court would be the one to designate someone to manage whatever assets we left behind for our child.

I worked with an attorney specializing in estate planning in my area to make sure that I had all of the documents necessary for proper estate planning.

There are many forms available on the internet that I could have used, but I did not feel comfortable using online forms, as rules and regulations vary from one state to another. I wanted to make sure my documents would be legally enforceable. Also, I met and worked with an attorney at no additional cost through employee benefits at work. However, I know several people who have done the research and used online forms. Whichever way you decide, you should make sure that your documents meet the legal requirements of where you live.

Wills are living documents. As we go through significant changes in life, we must remember to update our will—to ensure that it reflects our current situation and wishes.

Trust

A trust is a legal document that directs how your assets should be handled upon your death. A trust also designates a trustee to be the manager of the trust when you are no longer able.

With a revocable trust, as opposed to a nonrevocable trust, you can make changes to the trust without needing permission from the beneficiaries of the trust. You can modify, alter, or even void a revocable trust, which you cannot do with an irrevocable trust.

For that reason, a revocable trust is a more flexible option than a nonrevocable trust.

Revocable trusts are particularly attractive when you have assets to leave to your dependents or loved ones. Having a trust will allow them to bypass the probate process, which can be lengthy and costly. The cost of probate is often between 3 and 7 percent of the estate's size, and probate proceedings can take up to a year or two depending on how many parties are involved. During that time, the assets are usually frozen by the court.

When you set up a trust, you have more control over how and when your assets are distributed.

If you have young children, having a trust will help ensure they do not get all of their inheritance when they turn eighteen. You have the option to spread it out over some time. However, creating a trust can be expensive, generally costing 1,000 dollars or more to set up.

When beneficiaries have to go through probate, they cannot access their inheritance until the court authorizes the assets to be transferred to the beneficiaries. As such, if they rely on the estate to live, going through probate can put them in a challenging financial situation.

If you have assets, even if it is only your home, and if you have dependents, especially minor children, you should consider having a revocable trust.

Life insurance

Life insurance is a form of financial security that you purchase to provide financial support to one or more beneficiaries in case you were to pass away. It is a contract between yourself and an insurance company, in which you agree to pay the premiums, in exchange for a payment to your life insurance beneficiary. If you have a spouse or kids who rely on your income, it is a financial security that you should strongly consider. Dealing with the death of a parent or a spouse is a devastating experience. Being proactive in having life insurance would at least help ensure your loved ones will not have to struggle financially. It is a valuable piece of financial planning that can help you raise strong and financially secure kids.

There are two main types of life insurance you should know about: term life and whole life.

Term life insurance

Term life insurance provides specific financial coverage to your beneficiaries for the term of the policy (typically ranging between ten and thirty years), as long as you continue to make the premium payments. If you were to die during the term, your beneficiaries would receive the payout amount from the insurance company. There is no cash value associated with term life insurance unless you pass away during the term. However, because term life insurance is for a specific period, it is much more affordable than whole life insurance. As your children grow into independent adults, and as you and your spouse have accumulated enough assets, the need to have life insurance will decrease.

Whole life insurance

Whole life insurance provides a certain amount of financial coverage to your beneficiaries without a time limit, as long as you continue to make premium payments until maturity. Also, a portion of the premium payments that you make to the insurance company goes toward your policy's cash value.

Whole life insurance is significantly more expensive than term life insurance, sometimes up to fifteen times more expensive for similar term coverage.

Melissa, a friend of mine in her early thirties, was recently shopping for a 500,000-dollar life insurance policy. She received the two quotes below for a twenty-year term policy and whole life insurance policy. Melissa reached out to me as she was trying to decide which policy to pick.

	Term	Whole Life
Annual Premium	$-300	$-3,672
Expected value after 20 years	$-	$-105,000

Melissa received a twenty-year term life insurance annual quote of 300 dollars and a whole life insurance quote of 3,672 dollars. Also, the whole life policy has an expected cash value of 105,000 dollars after twenty years. In this instance, the whole life policy costs 3,372 dollars more per year than the term policy and 67,440 dollars over twenty years.

If Melissa were to invest the 3,372 dollars in a mutual fund or an exchange-traded fund every year, assuming a 7 percent rate of return, she could expect it to grow to approximately 146,000 dollars. This represents 42,000 dollars more or 40 percent over the expected cash value at the same time for the whole life insurance policy.

Whole life insurance is often presented as an investment opportunity. However, it is a poor long-term investment. It is wiser to get the coverage that you need in the form of term life insurance and invest the dollar difference whole life insurance would cost you.

Determining life insurance needs

There are two approaches to consider when looking into getting life insurance.

When it comes to life insurance needs, there are very two popular approaches. The first approach is income-based—aim to have at least ten to twelve times your annual income in life insurance coverage. For instance, if your income is 50,000 dollars a year, you should aim to have between 500,000 and 600,000 dollars of life insurance coverage.

Another approach to consider is getting a life insurance policy that is twenty-five times your annual expenses. For instance, if your annual expenses are 30,000 dollars a year, you should look into a policy of around 750,000 dollars.

I encourage you to estimate your life insurance needs with both approaches and determine how conservative you want to be. If you look at your finances and cannot get enough coverage under any of the two methods, you should get as much coverage as you can afford. The most important thing is to provide financial security to your loved ones in the event of your death. You can get additional insurance as your financial situation improves.

When to get life insurance

You should get life insurance coverage as early as possible. Life insurance is more affordable, the younger and healthier you are. As you get older, you are more susceptible to have health conditions, which is likely to increase your life insurance premiums. On average, life insurance premiums increase by about 8 to 10 percent every year of age.

Let us take my friend Melissa who received a quote of 300 dollars a year for a twenty-year term policy. If she were to wait ten more years to get life insurance, her annual premium is likely to increase by 478 dollars a year (778 dollars in premiums). This would translate into 9,560 in extra insurance premiums over the policy's twenty-year life. Also, during the ten years, Melissa's loved ones would be vulnerable if something were to happen.

I advise you to get life insurance coverage as soon as possible. You should only sign up for fixed annual premiums. This will ensure that you get a life insurance policy, and that your yearly premiums will stay the same for the rest of the policy.

Employer-provided life insurance

Some employers provide life insurance to their employees. Typically, there is a free life insurance coverage offered as part of your employee benefits. But, it is not enough, as it is usually one to two times an employee's salary. Employers also provide the option to purchase supplemental life insurance. However, it is in your best interest to explore life insurance outside of your employer, especially if you do not expect to stay with the same employer for the term of your policy.

Early in my professional career, I signed up for supplemental life insurance through my employer. But, a few years ago, I decided to get an individual life insurance policy.

Having life insurance coverage outside of your employer would help avoid a lapse in coverage if you were to switch jobs. If you were to decide to leave your employer, you would likely be presented with the option to convert your employer group life insurance policy to an individual life insurance policy, but it would likely be at a higher premium.

Also, you cannot predict what you will do ten years from now. You might decide to start your own business or to join a company that does not provide group life insurance. You would then have to get an individual policy, and your premium would be much higher as you would be ten years older.

It is worth getting a life insurance policy outside of your workplace while you are still young, if you like the option. I decided to get an individual twenty-year policy in my early thirties. It came at a premium of four dollars a month more than my employer's group policy (48 dollars extra a year), which was worth it. It gave me peace of mind to know that my life insurance was not tied to my workplace, so my premiums would stay the same for twenty-five years. If you are interested in switching from your employer's supplemental group policy to an individual policy, ensure that you are enrolled in the new policy before canceling the group policy.

Durable power of attorney for finances

A durable power of attorney for finances designates a person that you trust to handle your finances if you were unable to manage your finances due to being incapacitated. A durable power of attorney will automatically be enforceable if a medical doctor assesses that you are not capable of making your decisions, or physically unable to—for instance, if you are in a coma.

You should be very careful whom you give your financial power of attorney to as they would be able to make financial decisions on your behalf.

Usually, spouses have active powers of attorney for each other or designate an adult child. However, it is crucial to understand that only a durable power of attorney for finances would be valid if you were to become incapacitated or if you were to pass away. A typical financial power of attorney would automatically end if that were to happen. If you became incapacitated and did not have a durable power of attorney for finances in places, the court system will likely need to be involved in your financial affairs.

You can revoke your durable power of attorney for finances at any time as long you are of sound mind.

Healthcare power of attorney

A healthcare power of attorney or durable power of attorney for healthcare is a legal document that takes effect if you become incapable of making medical decisions for yourself.

When you have a durable power of attorney for health-care in place, you designate your spouse, adult child, or a person that you trust as your agent. Your agent will be responsible for making medical decisions on your behalf. Often, people overlook the importance of having a healthcare power of attorney in place. However, if you were to be incapacitated suddenly, a person you would not have chosen might decide for you.

You should consider a healthcare power of attorney as part of your estate planning. You can make changes to the document or revoke it as long as you are not mentally incapacitated.

Once a person already has an illness that leaves them mentally incapacitated, the process of getting a medical power of attorney is more complicated. The judicial system would need to be involved to ensure that it would be in your best interest.

According to the numbers published by the World Health Organization (WHO) in September 2019, there were approximately fifty million people worldwide with dementia, and an increase to eighty-two million people is expected by 2030. As much as we all want to believe that we will not need a healthcare power of attorney, it is best to continue to hope for the best but also be proactive by preparing for the worst.

Advance medical directive

An advance medical directive or advance healthcare directive is a legal document in which you specify which decisions you would like to take regarding your health, in the event you are incapacitated and unable to make the decisions for yourself. If you are unable to speak for yourself, the advance medical directive provides your loved ones with guidelines to follow regarding specific situations. An advance healthcare directive also allows you to address how you would like your end-of-life care to be handled. This type of directive includes addressing your views on the use of cardiopulmonary resuscitation (CPR), tube feeding, or even ventilators.

It is meant to help your loved ones make decisions regarding your medical care. However, if you would instead leave the decisions up to the healthcare agent you have chosen, a healthcare power of attorney should be sufficient.

Disability insurance

Most people overlook disability insurance as part of their financial plan. However, throughout the cost of your career, disability (short or long term) is more likely to happen than death. Approximately a quarter of professionals can expect to have a temporary disability of a year before retirement. Though disability can sometimes result from having an accident, it is more likely to be the result of an illness. Disability insurance will protect your income, and help you and your family cover your regular expenses and bills.

Many companies offer disability insurance. However, similar to life insurance, leaving the company would mean losing the policy. While having disability insurance through your employer is an excellent first step, also explore having an individual supplemental policy aligned with your needs.

Disability insurance can typically cover up to 70 percent of your income, depending on the policy. While short-term disability insurance is the most common, it will only replace a portion of your income for a short period, typically for up to six months. If you are unable to work for at least a year, long-term disability will start coverage after an elimination period** and replace up to a set percentage of your income for years, sometimes up to retirement.

---

* * The elimination period is a waiting period before a policyholder can receive long-term disability insurance benefits. Depending on the policy, it can be from several weeks to a few months.

Long-term disability is a more cost-effective protection than short-term disability in case of a loss of income due to a disability. A long-term disability policy will usually cost between 1 and 3 percent of your income. Short-term disability insurance often costs as much as long-term disability insurance for a much shorter coverage period. Disability insurance is an option to consider to add an extra layer of security to your financials.

CHAPTER 14
The Power of Community

Understanding the importance of coming together

"If you want to go fast, go alone. If you want to go far, go together." This African proverb illustrates why it is essential for Black people to unite and work together toward a common goal if we want to see real progress in the Black community.

The Black community has been destroyed and encouraged to separate over the years. Black people in America and Africa deserve reparations for all of the exploitation, trauma, and suffering we have had to endure. However, it is improbable that reparations will ever happen.

We cannot afford to wait on politicians to fix issues created by slavery, colonialism, or systemic racism.

The way forward for the Black community is together—through economic empowerment. We can accomplish so much as a community. We have done it in the past, and we can do it again.

Before the civil rights movement, Auburn Avenue, which expands over less than two miles, was home to Atlanta's emerging Black middle class. As was the case in most of the country, especially in southern states, African Americans were confined to specific areas of the city due to segregation laws. As a response to racism and social and economic restrictions, African Americans built an independent economic structure on Auburn Avenue, affectionately named "Sweet Auburn." Auburn Avenue hosted successful Black businesses, congregations, and social organizations. Alonzo Herndon, a formerly enslaved successful barbershop owner and entrepreneur, was Atlanta's first black millionaire. In 1905, Alonzo Herndon founded Atlanta Life Insurance Company, the first financial institution on Auburn Avenue. Over the next fifteen years, other financial institutions like Standard Life Insurance Company and Citizens Trust Bank also opened in the Auburn District, catering to underserved Black entrepreneurs and homeowners. A century later, Atlanta Life Insurance Company and Citizens Trust Bank are still successful businesses. Described by *Fortune* magazine as "the richest Negro street in the world" in 1956, Auburn Avenue was renowned for being an example of Black entrepreneurial success and wealth. Auburn Avenue started experiencing a decline in the 1960s, around the end of segregation. Businesses and residents began moving to other parts of the city. The Auburn District was later split into two as a result of highway construction, and crime started to rise in the area. Sweet Auburn was designated as a national landmark in 1976 and is home to the Martin Luther King Jr. Center. There have been multiple attempts to revive Sweet Auburn, with more promising efforts over the past five years.

In 1906, O.W. Gurley, a Black educator and landowner, purchased forty acres of land in Tulsa, Oklahoma, which later became Greenwood. At the time, many African Americans from the South migrated to escape segregationist laws. O.W. Gurley's vision was to create a community for Black people to thrive. Other successful Black business people subsequently moved to Greenwood. J.B. Stratford, a formerly enslaved lawyer and activist, moved to Greenwood and built a luxury hotel. Like O.W. Gurley, he believed that Black people had a better chance of success if they pooled their resources together. By 1920, Greenwood was self-reliant and had over six hundred businesses. Greenwood, also known as the Black "Wall Street," had its school system, shops, restaurants, post office, banks, churches, grocery stores, hotels, clothing stores, barbershops, libraries, and hospitals. More than ten thousand Black Americans lived in Greenwood, including doctors, lawyers, business owners, and less affluent Black people. In Greenwood, the average income for Black families exceeded the minimum wage. Even though there were only two airports in the state of Oklahoma at the time, there were six Black families in Greenwood who owned their own airplanes. The Black "Wall Street" was thriving, and at that time, a dollar would circulate thirty-six times before leaving the community.

On May 30, 1921, a Black teenager named Dick Rowland was accused of attacking Sarah Page, a White woman, in an elevator in the *Tulsa Tribune*. Sarah Page, who initially said that she had been sexually assaulted by Dick Roland, quickly recanted her story to say that Roland tripped and fell onto her. Dick Roland was still arrested and held in a courthouse cell.

On May 31, 1921, a large group of armed White men gathered outside the courthouse, demanding that the sheriff hand over Dick Rowland. That evening, a group of armed Black men went to the courthouse. There were rumors of a possible lynching of Dick Rowland, and they wanted to offer help to guard the Black teenager. The sheriff declined the request from both groups. Shortly after, a group of armed White men tried to break into the National Guard. The two groups exchanged shots. The Black men, who were outnumbered, went back to the Greenwood District. Later that evening, thousands of White supremacists, many of them armed, invaded Greenwood.

They killed hundreds of Black men, women, and children, and destroyed most of the businesses and the houses in Greenwood. Black Wall Street was destroyed, leaving 1.8 million dollars in damages (about 30 million in today's dollars), and close to the entire population of Greenwood homeless. Charges against Dick Rowland were later dropped, but the media and local politicians described the Tulsa riot as an uprising started by "lawless Blacks." The Tulsa Race Riot Commission suggested that the people who lost property receive reparations. The Commission also recommended the economic revitalization of the Greenwood community. Unfortunately, the survivors of the Greenwood riot never received reparations.

Black residents of Greenwood pulled their resources together to rebuild. By 1922, eight businesses had reopened in Greenwood, and all of the homes had been rebuilt. However, Greenwood was never able to recover fully. With the end of segregation and the urban renewal projects of the sixties and seventies, businesses in Greenwood began to decline. The Black Wall Street was created by Black people, as a result of discrimination, to provide a safe environment for Black people to thrive. It is an example of what we can do together as a community if we collaborate.

Black Wall Street and Auburn Avenue are only two of the examples of the level of wealth and success Black entrepreneurs were able to accomplish despite segregation and racial discrimination. It is proof of concept that when the Black community decides to work together, we can find success even if the system is built against us.

In his last speech delivered on April 3, 1968, in Memphis, Tennessee, "I have been to the Mountaintop," Dr. Martin Luther King Jr. promoted a message of empowerment for the Black community through economics. "Collectively, we are richer than all the nations in the world, with the exception of nine," Dr. King said. "We have an annual income of more than thirty billion dollars a year, which is more than all of the exports of the United States, and more than the national budget of Canada. Did you know that? That is power right there if we know how to pool it."

Fifty years later, the speech resonates even more. In 2019, the Black community's purchasing power in the United States alone was 1.3 trillion dollars.[I] Unfortunately, according to the results of the Empowerment Experiment,[II] less than 3 percent of our purchasing dollars is spent in the Black community. According to the study, if the Black community-directed 10 percent of its purchasing power to Black-owned companies directly and supported Black vendors, agents, franchises, or larger firms, it could create up to one million jobs for the community.

There have been a lot of claims regarding how long a dollar lasts in the Black community. *Trigger Warning*,[III] a documentary by Killer Mike released in 2019, highlights that a dollar only stays in the Black community for six hours, compared to seventeen days in the White community, twenty days in the Jewish community, and thirty days in the Asian community. In his documentary, Killer Mike committed to only buying Black for twenty-four hours, which came with challenges.

There are several organizations to help find Black businesses and encourage buying Black—Official Black Wall Street Black-Owned Businesses Directory, We Buy Black, Buy from a Black Woman, or Buy Black Movement are just a few.

Though many of us do not live in predominately Black neighborhoods, most of us have access to the internet. Committing 10 percent or more of our spending to the Black community seems like a reasonable undertaking. It might not happen overnight, but we can start with small steps. Black spending power will continue to grow with time; how we spend our money to rebuild the Black community is up to us. However, the support of the Black community is not restricted to where a person lives.

Pulling resources together to invest and build wealth is also something we need to do more of in the Black community. Whether it is to purchase real estate, start business ventures, or buy stakes in Black-owned start-ups, pulling resources with family, friends, and other investors to build wealth is something we need to be more intentional about doing in the Black community.

In 2000, Ghana passed the "Right of Abode" law, allowing any person of African descent to apply for the right to stay in Ghana indefinitely. In 2018, Nana Akufo-Addo, the president of Ghana, declared 2019 the "Year of Return." The year 2019 marked four hundred years since the arrival of enslaved Africans in America. The initiative was to encourage people of African descent to visit Ghana and invest in the country. Hundreds of thousands more people traveled to Ghana in 2019 compared to the prior year. Ghana granted Ghanaian citizenship to approximately one hundred African Americans and Afro-Caribbeans as part of the "Year of Return." The effects of the initiative also boosted the country's economy by close to two billion dollars.[IV] Ghana's most recent initiative follows in the footsteps of pan-African leaders like Kwame Nkrumah and W.E.B. Du Bois, who encouraged Black people all over the world to unify and work toward a common interest.

In today's society, minorities like the Jewish or Asian communities have shown us that being united leads to more success for the community. It is time that we apply the learnings from people like O.W. Gurley and choose to be more united as a community. We can make a more conscious effort at the individual level to support the Black community by not only targeting how we spend our money, but also by donating to organizations creating positive change in Black communities. We can save ourselves through education and working together. We can improve our fate and achieve success as a community. When we organize and understand that together our voice is much stronger, we can exert our power and bring about social change.

CHAPTER 15

Key Financial Mistakes to Avoid

Avoiding common obstacles to financial success

This chapter focuses on eleven common financial mistakes. Avoiding these mistakes will help you save a lot of money and build wealth for your family.

Failing to pay yourself first

Paying yourself first means saving a set portion of your income—before paying your bills, buying groceries, or doing anything else. Often, people, especially young people, tend to spend their money and only save whatever is left. This practice typically results in saving less than you could if you had been intentional about your savings. At the end of the month, you wonder where your money went—when you should be directing your money toward the right path to wealth building.

Every month, the first bill that you pay should be to yourself. To make it easy to pay yourself first, you can automate this process by having a certain percentage of your income automatically directed to a specific account, separated from your day-to-day accounts. This set percentage of income that you put aside first can be used to build your emergency fund, and to save for retirement or other important projects.

Failing to negotiate your salary properly

Black people are used to working twice as hard to get half as much recognition as White counterparts. When we receive employment offers from companies that only have a few spots for people who look like us, many of us fail to negotiate our salary. We often react this way because we are aware that most of our brothers and sisters will not have similar opportunities. But the reality is that we short-change ourselves in the process.

In 2016, the Pew Research Center published an article entitled "Racial, gender wage gaps persist in the U.S. despite some progress." According to the data, Black people's hourly earnings are 25 percent less than their White counterparts.[1] Black women get paid, on average, 65 cents for every dollar that a White male counterpart makes—no matter the position. Though employment discrimination based on a person's race or gender is illegal, it still exists today.

To get employment opportunities as minorities, we have to be excellent. We should not accept the first offer that we receive out of fear. Sometimes, we mistakenly believe that the most important thing is to make sure that we get our foot in the door—and that we will have an opportunity to renegotiate later. But, in most cases, when you fail to negotiate your salary when you join a company, you limit your long-term earning potential. Your best chance to see a significant increase in your salary is when you first join a company. Once you are in, most companies have caps, limiting how much your salary can increase at once.

Let us say that you receive a job offer for a salary of 65,000 dollars. Let us say that you stayed at the company for six years and received a promotion every three years, but the company caps salary increases at 15 percent. During the years you were not promoted, you received a merit increase of 3 percent. Let us look at the scenario if you negotiated your entry salary, and let us look at the situation if you did not negotiate.

Option 1: Accept the offer

Year 1: 60,000 dollars
Year 2: 61,800 dollars after a 3 percent merit increase
Year 3: 71,070 dollars after promotion capped at 15 percent increase
Year 4: 73,202 dollars after a 3 percent merit increase
Year 5: 75,398 dollars after a 3 percent merit increase
Year 6: 86,708 dollars after promotion capped at 15 percent

Total earnings in 6 years = 428,178 dollars.

Option 2: Negotiate the offer

Year 1: 66,000 dollars
Year 2: 67,980 dollars after a 3 percent merit increase
Year 3: 78,177 dollars after promotion capped at 15 percent increase
Year 4: 80,522 dollars after a 3 percent merit increase
Year 5: 82,938 dollars after a 3 percent merit increase
Year 6: 95,379 dollars after promotion capped at 15 percent

Total earnings in 6 years = 470,996 dollars

Impact of not negotiating: 42,818.

If you stayed at that company for six years, you would lose close to 43,000 dollars of earnings—71 percent of your initial salary—because you accepted the first offer that you received. If you stay with the company longer than six years, then the impact would be even more significant. Your best option to increase your income would be to leave the company to get a nice pay bump. Unfortunately, sometimes we tend to repeat the same mistake, because the first offer is much more than we are currently making.

The first step toward adequately negotiating your salary is to do your research. Some websites can provide a salary range for the position that you are pursuing. Applications like Glassdoor or Payscale can give you an idea of the salary range for the position in your specific geographic area. Though it will not be exact, it is a great starting point. However, keep in mind that it is best to avoid asking salary-related questions until the recruiter or hiring manager has brought up the topic.

Another important negotiation tactic is not to disclose your compensation information until you know the salary range and total compensation for the position. You can avoid answering the question directly when or if a recruiter asks, but take that opportunity to then ask about the salary range for the job. It is preferable to have that information before you disclose your salary, if asked to do so. It will make a considerable difference during the negotiation process.

Borrowing money at a high-interest rate

People are often more concerned with fitting a monthly payment within their budget than they are with the cost of borrowing money.

As seen in previous chapters, minorities are often targeted when it comes to predatory lending. Researching interest rates for the loan that you are interested in is an essential step to ensure you do not fall victim to that. Paying close attention to interest rates will help manage your financing cost. Failing to do so can put you at risk of predatory lending and in a tough financial situation. Do your research, so you already know which interest rate to expect before borrowing money.

Living above your means

Living above your means is spending more money than you bring in each month. Living above your means is financing your lifestyle through credit cards or borrowing money. Living above your means is expensive. When you rely on credit cards and loans to pay your bills and cover your expenses, it comes at a financing cost. The cost of financing will keep you in debt and slow you down on the way to financial freedom. Consider saving for large purchases until you can pay for them outright. Living below your means is a much better alternative—it is also a necessary step to creating financial security. Knowing how much money you make after taxes, paying yourself first, creating a plan for your money, and spending less money than you make are essential to building financial freedom.

Failing to plan for unexpected expenses

Failing to plan for unexpected expenses can result in a personal financial crisis. The 2019 COVID-19 pandemic resulted in millions of people losing their jobs overnight in the United States, and many states were overwhelmed, which caused a delay in the processing of unemployment claims. Predicting a pandemic is highly unlikely for the average person—but it is safe to assume that something unexpected will happen in the future. In this instance, having money set aside would have helped to get through the first few weeks or months of the pandemic. Planning for the unexpected can buy time to figure out what to do next—without worrying about being able to pay all your bills or losing your home. A common rule of thumb is that there is a 25 percent chance that you will face unforeseen expenses every year. Planning for unexpected expenses can save you from a financial crisis.

Trying to time the stock market

Timing the stock market is deciding to buy and sell stocks based on your predictions of market movements. When you try to time the market, you may get lucky once or twice—but making it an investment strategy does not work.

The stock market is unpredictable—it might go up after you decide to sell to minimize your losses or continue to increase after you sell to capitalize on your gains. If your strategy is to time the market, you might get out of the market too early, or risk being out of the market when it unexpectedly surges. Timing the market can lead you to make emotional decisions as you worry about prices being too high or too low.

A healthier investment strategy is to dollar cost average your money into the stock market. Historical data shows that if you continue to invest little by little, whether the market is up or down, you will win in the long run. Under this strategy, you understand that the stock market will always go back up— you are just unaware of when it will happen.

Blindly trusting a financial advisor

Before investing money in the stock market, a great present you can give yourself is taking the time to learn the basics of the stock market. Understanding the basics is vital to ensure you never give up control to your financial advisor. Trusting your advisor blindly leaves you at risk—like the many people who were victims of Bernie Madoff.

In reality, most people do not need a financial advisor. Financial advisors are expensive, often charging between 1 and 2 percent of assets under management. In most cases, financial advisors do not provide enough value to justify the fee. Many will place your money in mutual funds or exchange-traded funds—which you can easily do on your own if you learn the basics of investing.

Financial advisors rarely help their customers beat the market—less than 10 percent of fund managers tend to do it. Putting your money in the S&P 500 is likely to provide similar or higher returns than using a financial advisor.

If you are not comfortable going that route, another option to explore is a Robo-advisor. For a small fee, companies like Bloom or Betterment offer that option to help you select funds and rebalance your portfolio regularly.

Even though financial advisors can be expensive over the long run, a good financial advisor is someone who can be very useful in times of market turmoil. They can talk you through tough times—and for some people, that alone is worth paying a fee.

If you want to hire a human advisor, consider hiring a fee-only advisor. It is also crucial to check the potential advisors' credentials and complaint records and conduct interviews to find an advisor that is a good fit for you. It is essential to know how your potential advisor is compensated. Do you see any potential conflict of interest? Do they speak in terms that you can understand? Your advisor should provide financial advice, but you should manage your own money and sign your own checks. One of the most important things to remember when it comes to hiring people to help you manage your money is that you should never relinquish control over your money.

Failing to discuss finances before marriage

Money is one of the leading causes of divorce—couples should have honest conversations about finances before getting married. It is essential to openly discuss your financials, including debt and credit, before marrying someone. Sharing your views about money and how you are planning to handle money within your marriage is equally important. In a marriage, your spouse should add to your efforts—together, the two of you should build a more solid financial foundation. Being married to a financially irresponsible person or someone who does not understand the importance of having financial goals is likely to become a burden. You should ensure that you and your future spouse agree on how to handle your money to build financial wealth together.

Failing to teach the fundamentals of money to kids

Your kids will learn money lessons as they grow up. It is essential to have money conversations with your Kings and Queens throughout their childhood and as they become young adults.

Kids also learn money habits from watching their parents—it is important to lead by example. If you want your children to develop a good relationship with money, then it is critical to teach them the fundamentals of money before someone else does.

When children grow up understanding hard work and delayed gratification, they are less likely to use credit cards to pay for something they cannot afford. Kids should understand the importance of being proactive as opposed to being reactive with their money. They should know the value of compound interest and of giving back. Kids should learn the dangers of debt—including student loans. Teaching your kids about money is preparing them to become economically self-sufficient in the future. It helps them avoid financial mistakes that could cost them years to fix—and set them on the path toward financial freedom.

Postponing retirement savings

Saving for retirement should be a priority when you begin your professional career. Early on, even if you can only afford to set aside 1 percent of your income toward retirement, you should do it. Developing the habit early is crucial to continuing the behavior. Thanks to the value of compound interest, even a ten dollar contribution will matter in forty years. Taking advantage of any free money that you get from your company toward your retirement is essential. When you prepare for your retirement, you send a signal to your children of how important it is to plan for the long-term. Saving for retirement is also a way to alleviate your children's worries in the future.

Failing to pay the IRS on time

Filing and paying your taxes should be at the top of your priority list. In the United States, most adults must file their taxes. As of 2020, the minimum income requirement to file a tax return varies from 12,200 to 24,400, depending on your filing status. It is essential to know where you stand. If you think you might be in the minority of people who do not have to file a return, you should check the requirements every year. That is the only way you will know whether or not you owe taxes to the Internal Revenue Service. Not filing a tax return without checking that information is not worth the consequences that you may have to face for failing to pay the IRS.

The Internal Revenue Service does not have a time limit on the collection of taxes, penalties, and interest for the years you did not file your taxes.

Tax evasion is the intentional nonpayment or underpayment of tax liabilities due to the IRS. In addition to paying back taxes, you will have to pay interest and penalties and risk going to jail for up to five years.

There are too many examples of prominent Black figures who have had tax problems to know that you should take this matter seriously. While some were able to sort their issues by paying what they owed to the IRS, others also had to go to prison.

It is a much wiser alternative to file your taxes and pay what you owe to the IRS. It is also important to note that a taxpayer is responsible for the accuracy of their tax return. You should review the numbers before signing your tax return if you use a CPA or other tax practitioners to prepare your taxes.

FINAL THOUGHTS

My journey to writing this book is ending while Black Lives Matter protests are happening around the world. The catalyst behind the uprising was the murder of George Floyd, one more Black person who unjustly died as a result of systemic racism. A few weeks prior, Ahmaud Arbery was lynched by White supremacists while he was jogging, and police officers killed Breonna Taylor while she was asleep in her home. The common theme in all three situations was that the people who committed the crimes were not charged until there was a public outcry.

With those events, the Black community joined forces to demand justice for the unjust killings. By joining forces to organize and protest, and with the help of allies from other communities, Ahmaud Arbery and George Floyd's killers were charged for murder, and Breonna Taylor's case was reopened. Protests against police brutality and in support of the Black Lives Matter movement have now spread worldwide.

It is a testament to the power of coming together. However, it also highlights the importance of having a voice. Black people have been voiceless for far too long. We cannot continue to be reactive to injustice.

The current climate reinforces the need for us to strengthen our voice through the economic empowerment of the Black community.

We have to teach financial literacy to our kids so they can be empowered. The Black community needs to come together. We cannot wait for the system to change. We have to build our communities by being intentional about how we spend our money.

We can build generational wealth, just like other communities before us. We have to instill habits in our children early on to help them become strong and financially secure adults.

ACKNOWLEDGMENTS

Thank you to my parents. You have shown me the definition of unconditional love, integrity, and sacrifice. You taught by example and always stayed by my side, even when you did not agree with my decisions. I can never repay you for everything that you have done for me. Thank you for encouraging my love for reading by allowing me to read books from your library when I was a child. I love you both.

To my husband: Jay. I never knew a love like this. I am so grateful for your love and partnership. I am blessed to be married to someone who supports me and encourages me to go after my dreams, no matter how big they are. Thank you for being my rock, and my number one supporter. Thank you for encouraging me to see this project through. You are the definition of a ride or die.

To my children: Cecilia, Aya, and Kuimi. Being your mother has truly been the greatest gift of my life. Your presence has shifted my existence. You inspire me, you challenge me, and you make me laugh like there is no tomorrow.

To Nya and McKenzie. Your birth has enhanced my life. It is an honor to watch you grow. I look forward to spending more time with you and guiding you through life. I cannot wait to see you unlock the greatness that you have inside of you.

To Raphaële, it is hard to believe that you were our little shrimp a few years ago. You were the first newborn baby that I held, and now you are growing into a young lady. Remember that sky is the limit.

To my siblings, thank you for my amazing childhood memories. Thank you for the support, tough love, and sense of humor, even when the jokes were at my expense.

To my sisters: Big Munchkin, Aurore, and Dr. Z. God truly blessed me by giving me three exceptional sisters and role models. Thank you for being patient with me. Thank you for always having my back.

Aurore and Dr. Z, so much of me is you. As long as I am alive, you will live through me.

Big Munchkin, you were heavily invested in this project. Thank you for seeing the vision and bringing the cover to life. Thank you for always believing in me. What is understood does not need to be said. I would do anything for you. Thank you for giving me Nya and for embracing me with all of my stubbornness.

To my brothers: Franck and Bayes. Thank you for protecting me and supporting me.

Franck , I can't thank you enough for going above and beyond to promote this project..

To A, my soul sister. Thank you for believing in the vision, and for pulling me up when I am down. Thank you for the soulful conversations and free editing. You have no idea how special you are.

To Julz, thank you for the role you played as my cheerleader for this project. You truly are a gem. We have come so far together. Thank you for your sisterhood and for always praying for me. Thank you for my babies.

Thank you to all of my family—cousins, nephews, aunties, and uncles who have helped raise me.

To my friends, thank you for bearing with me through all of my changes. Thank you for supporting me.

To all of my mentors, thank you for the guidance and for believing in me.

To everyone who inspired this book, thank you.

NOTES

Prologue

I "The Economic Impact of Closing the Racial Wealth Gap," McKinsey & Company, August 2019.
II "The Effects of the 1930s HOLC 'Redlining' Maps," Federal Reserve Bank of Chicago, Daniel Aaronson, Daniel Hartley, and Bhashkar Mazumder, February 2019.

Chapter 2: Teaching Self-Love

I "AC 360 Kids on Race: The Hidden Picture," CNN.

Chapter 3: Teaching Gratitude

I "Gratitude Is Associated with Greater Levels of Protective Factors and Lower Levels of Risks in African American Adolescents," Mindy Ma, Jeffrey L. Kibler, and Kaye Sly, August 2013.

Chapter 4: Teaching Solid Financial Habits Early

I "Report on the Economic Well-Being of U.S. Households in 2019, Featuring Supplemental Data from April 2020," Board of Governors of the Federal Reserve System, May 2020.

Chapter 8: Managing Debt

I "Consumer-Lending Discrimination in the FinTech Era," Robert Bartlett, Adair Morse, Richard Stanton, and Nancy Wallace, November 2019.
II "Quarterly Report on Household Debt and Credit (2019 Q3)," November 2019, Federal Reserve Bank of New York.
III "Status and Trends in the Education of Racial and Ethnic Groups 2018," The National Center for Education Statistics (NCES) of the U.S. Department of Education, February 2019.
IV "Black-White Disparity in Student Loan Debt More Than Triples after Graduation," Brookings, Judith Scott-Clayton, October 2016.

V "Quicksand: Borrowers of Color and the Student Debt Crisis," National Association for the Advancement of Colored People (NAACP) and the Center for Responsible Lending (CRL), July 2019.

VI "Federal Reserve Statistical Release Consumer Credit April 2020," June 5, 2020.

VII "Used Vehicles Continue to Be the Preferred Option for Car Shoppers," Experian PLC, December 5, 2019. "Federal Reserve Statistical Release Consumer Credit April 2020," June 5, 2020.

VIII "Car Depreciation, How Much Will a New Car Lose," Carfax, November 9, 2018.

IX "Fast Cash and Payday Loans," April Economic Research Federal Reserve Bank of St. Louis, Jeannette N. Bennett, April 2019.

X "Young Adults, Student Debt and Economic Well-Being," Richard Fry, Pew Research Center, May 14, 2014.

XI "Thinking of Buying a House? Here's How Much Home You Can Buy for $200K in Every State," Grant Suneson, March 16, 2020.

XII "Current Interest Rates by Financial Product, Mortgages," Holden Lewis, NerdWallet.com.

Chapter 10: Saving for the Long Run

I "Retirement Perspectives, Income Replacement in Retirement," T. Rowe Price, May 2019.

II "Report on the Economic Well-Being of U.S. Households in 2018," Board of Governors of the Federal Reserve System, May 2019.

III "Q1 2019 Retirement Analysis: Account Balances Rebound from DIP in Q4, While Savings Rates Hit Record Levels," Fidelity Investments, May 9, 2019.

IV "Starting Salary for Class of 2018 Hovers near $51,000," National Association of Colleges and Employers (NACE), July 10, 2019.

V "Scholarships and Grants for College Students," Debt.Org., Max Fay.

VI "5 Myths about Athletic Scholarships," U.S. News, Deborah Ziff Soriana and Emma Kerr, March 9, 2020.

VII "Trends in Higher Education Series, Trends in College Pricing 2019," College Board, November 2019.

VIII "A Look at Wealth 2019, Millenial Millionaires," Coldwell Banker, October 16, 2019.

Chapter 11: Work Ethic and Entrepreneurship

I "Global Entrepreneurship Index," Global Entrepreneurship and Development Index (GEDI), 2019.
II "The Tapestry of Black Business Ownership in America: Untapped Opportunities for Success," Association for Enterprise Opportunity, March 20, 2017.
III "Minority Entrepreneurs," U.S. Senate Committee on Small Business & Entrepreneurship, 2019.
IV "Black or African American Owned Businesses in the United States," U.S. Small Business Administration Office of Advocacy, May 1, 2016.

Chapter 12: Building Multiple Sources of Income

I "Rich Habits: The Daily Success Habits of the Wealthy Individuals," Thomas Corley, August 2009.

Chapter 14: The Power in Community

I "It's in the Bag, Black Consumers' Path to Purchase," Nielsen, September 12, 2019.
II "The Empowerment Experiment," is a yearlong effort conducted by the Anderson family in partnership with Northwestern University's elite Kellogg Graduate School of Management. The experiment was to prove, research, and analyze economic leakage and the potential impact of self-help economics/conscious consumerism on a mass scale.
III Trigger Warning is a documentary released in 2019 exploring social issues affecting the Black community in America.
IV "'Year of Return' Activities Bring $1.9 Billion into Ghana's Economy," DeAnna Taylor, Travel Noire, December 17, 2019.

Chapter 15: Key Financial Mistakes to Avoid

I "Racial, Gender Wage Gaps Persist in the U.S. Despite Some Progress," Pew Research Center, July 1, 2016.

ABOUT THE AUTHOR

Anne-Lyse Wealth began her career as a CPA working for a "Big Four" Public Accounting Firm. She is the founder of the personal finance and personal development site, DreamofLegacy.com.

Before embarking on her journey to increase financial literacy in the Black community, she had a ten-plus years finance career gaining experience in five different industries, from start-ups to *Fortune* 500 companies.

After identifying a personal finance knowledge gap among Black professionals, Anne-Lyse Wealth started educating her friends, family, and coworkers on the subject.

As her interest in personal finance increased, she noticed the lack of books to provide financial education to the Black community. With her first book, Anne-Lyse strives to help the Black community to have a better relationship with money and build generational wealth.

Made in the USA
Columbia, SC
19 January 2021